ISLINGTON W

Th
Bc

. . . .

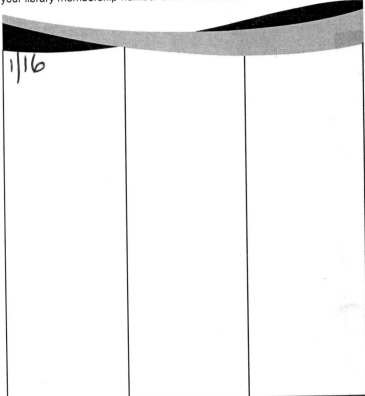

1/16

Islington Libraries

020 7527 6900   www.islington.gov.uk/libraries

PEARSON

At Pearson, we believe in learning – all kinds of learning for all kinds of people. Whether it's at home, in the classroom or in the workplace, learning is the key to improving our life chances.

That's why we're working with leading authors to bring you the latest thinking and best practices, so you can get better at the things that are important to you. You can learn on the page or on the move, and with content that's always crafted to help you understand quickly and apply what you've learned.

If you want to upgrade your personal skills or accelerate your career, become a more effective leader or more powerful communicator, discover new opportunities or simply find more inspiration, we can help you make progress in your work and life.

Pearson is the world's leading learning company. Our portfolio includes the Financial Times and our education business, Pearson International.

Every day our work helps learning flourish, and wherever learning flourishes, so do people.

To learn more, please visit us at **www.pearson.com/uk**

The Interview Book

How to prepare and perform at your best in any interview

Third edition

James Innes

Harlow, England • London • New York • Boston • San Francisco • Toronto • Sydney • Auckland • Singapore • Hong Kong
Tokyo • Seoul • Taipei • New Delhi • Cape Town • São Paulo • Mexico City • Madrid • Amsterdam • Munich • Paris • Milan

PEARSON EDUCATION LIMITED
Edinburgh Gate
Harlow CM20 2JE
United Kingdom
Tel: +44 (0)1279 623623
Web: www.pearson.com/uk

First edition published 2009 (print)
Second edition published 2012 (print and electronic)
Third edition published 2016

ISBN: 978-1-292-08651-4 (print)
         978-1-292-08653-8 (PDF)
         978-1-292-08652-1 (eText)
         978-1-292-08654-5 (ePub)

British Library Cataloguing-in-Publication Data
A catalogue record for the print edition is available from the British Library

Library of Congress Cataloging-in-Publication Data
Names: Innes, James, 1975- author.
Title: The interview book : how to prepare and perform at your best in any interview /
  James Innes.
Description: Third edition. | Harlow, United Kingdom : Pearson Education, 2016. | Includes
  bibliographical references and index.
Identifiers: LCCN 2015035997 | ISBN 9781292086514 (pbk.)
Subjects: LCSH: Employment interviewing.
Classification: LCC HF5549.5.I6 I55 2016 | DDC 650.14/4—dc23
LC record available at http://lccn.loc.gov/2015035997

10 9 8 7 6 5 4 3 2 1
20 19 18 17 16

Cover design by redeyoffdesign.com, cover image © Rodin Anton/ Shutterstock

Print edition typeset in 10/13pt Mundo Sans Pro by Lumina Datamatics
Printed and bound in Malaysia (CTP-PJB)

NOTE THAT ANY PAGE CROSS REFERENCES REFER TO THE PRINT EDITION

Dedication

This book is dedicated to my brother, Christian – for showing me the meaning of determination and the value of patience! And for inspiring me to make the very most of the chances life has granted me.

Half of the author's royalties for this book will go to Down Syndrome Education International (registered charity number 1062823), a charity whose applied research and practical support transform the lives of many thousands of children around the world. **Every year, approximately 1,000 babies are born with Down's syndrome in the UK alone**. I encourage my readers to join me in supporting this important cause. Donations can be made online at **www.justgiving.com/dseinternational**

Contents

About the author

James Innes is the founder and chairman of The CV Centre® – the UK's leading CV consultancy (**www.CVCentre.co.uk**) and part of the James Innes Group.

Following nearly two decades of experience heading up The CV Centre®, James is widely considered to be one of the UK's leading careers experts.

James regularly participates at recruitment fairs and conferences as a sought-after guest speaker, as well as being interviewed on TV and radio.

He is the author of a number of best-selling careers books. His current works are: *The CV Book*, *The Cover Letter Book*, *The Interview Book*, *The Interview Question & Answer Book* and *Ultimate New Job*.

Acknowledgements

I would like to thank all of my colleagues and clients at The CV Centre®, both present and past. Without them it would clearly not have been possible for me to write *The Interview Book*. In particular, I would like to thank our Chief Executive Officer, Andy Dalziel, Managing Editor, Katy Wilson as well as Amanda Jones and Linda Savill and our former Director of UK Operations, Susan Staley.

I would additionally like to thank Richard Day, our former Director of Technology and Peter Anders Hvass, our Chief Technology Officer, for their significant contributions to the online elements of this book, also Kirk Hullis, our Chief Marketing Officer, for his work on the promotion of the book.

Special thanks go to the team at Pearson Education, in particular Melanie Carter, Eloise Cook, Paul East, Lisa Robinson, Lesley Pummell, Dhanya Ramesh and the editorial services team at Lumina Datamatics and Emma Steel. I couldn't have had better publishers behind me.

Assistance in checking and correcting the text was also provided by Don Elkins, Elisabeth Elkins and Malcolm Innes.

Finally, I would like to thank my wife, Delphine Innes, and my daughter, Aleyna Innes, for their love and support and their toleration of my frequently working very excessively long hours! Je vous aime...

Publisher's acknowledgements

The questions on page 66 are reproduced from Edenborough (2009) *Brilliant Psychometric Tests*, Pearson Prentice Hall, © Pearson Education Limited 2009.

An apology in advance ...

It is impossible to write a book of this nature in such a way that all of the content will be perfectly suited to everyone. My readers range from manual workers to senior executives, to office staff and those who work in retail. Some will work in a team; some won't. Some will have a boss; some will be the boss.

I've done my best to deliver a book which covers, as much as possible, all the different circumstances my readers might be in and all the different issues they might have to face. But there will inevitably be sections which don't apply to your own circumstances or where the focus is either above or below your level in the hierarchy. I can only apologise for this and hope you'll be kind enough to forgive me. My advice is to take what you need and to leave the rest.

How to use this book

There's no doubt about it; this book covers a lot of ground.

However, I appreciate that you may well have an interview to attend later today and simply might not have the time to read everything. I have therefore provided a 'fast track' below by listing the top 15 questions that people ask me about interviews. This should help you to quickly and easily answer the vast majority of the points that are troubling you.

Once you've found the answers to your questions, before heading off for your interview, make sure you spare five minutes to read Part 8: My five top tips for interview success. If you only had time to read two pages of *The Interview Book*, these are the pages I would most like you to have taken the time to read. They encapsulate the most important principles that I cover in the book. Make an effort to accommodate all these when preparing for your interview and you'll immediately be well above average.

I'd also recommend that you take time to have a good look at Chapter 19: The ten questions you're most likely to be asked. You are absolutely certain to get asked at least some of these questions (or variations of them), if not the whole lot.

The top 15 questions that people ask me about interviews

Right, if you're short on time and need answers fast then this section is for you.

No, I'm not talking about the questions *you* might be asked at interview. I'm talking about the questions *you'd* most like to ask *me* about interviews.

The chances are you've got at least one – if not more – of the following questions on your mind.

I have compiled this list based on the questions we most frequently get asked at The CV Centre®. It contains the top 15 most common questions concerned job hunters ask about interviews; the questions that come up every single day. If you're reading this book then it's more than likely that you will be asking yourself many of the same questions.

Each question is listed alongside details of where in this book you can find the answers you are looking for.

All the answers to these questions and many more can be found within *The Interview Book*. And if you have a question to which you can't find the answer then why not visit our website: **www.jamesinn.es**

The top 15 questions

1 What sort of things should I be reading up on before my interview?

Chapter 2 Researching the job

Chapter 3 Researching the organisation

2 What can I do to calm my nerves and be more confident in myself and my abilities?

Chapter 4 Mental preparation

3 What should I wear?

Chapter 5 Presentation

4 What's all this about body language?

Chapter 6 Body language

5 What's really important to remember on the day?

Chapter 7 The big day

6 How can I make a really strong first impression?

Chapter 8 First impressions count

7 What can I expect to happen at my interview?

Chapter 10 Classic one-on-one interviews

8 How should I handle a panel interview?

Chapter 11 Panel interviews

9 What are competency-based interviews?

Chapter 12 Competency-based, behavioural and situational interviews

10 How can I prepare for psychometric/aptitude tests?

Chapter 13 Psychometric and aptitude tests

11 I have been asked to give a presentation. What's the best format?

Chapter 14 Presentations

PART **1**

PLANNING, PREPARATION AND ORGANISATION: A WINNING STRATEGY

Chapter **1**

....

Why are interviews so important?

Dear Reader,

Why do some people almost always get the job they want?

Because they know precisely how to *truly excel* at interview!

Years of experience as a coach working clients and preparing them to truly excel at interview have enabled me to share my knowledge and expertise and help you to excel at interview.

Once your CV has been prepared and you have sent off your applications, the next stage to focus on, in securing the job you want, is the interview phase.

So you've been invited for interview

Your CV has been successful and you have been invited for interview. What next? People often think, well I'll just turn up and be myself, which is fine, but it won't get you the job! Remember: You are up against numerous other candidates, so you need to stand out and make an impact. To do that you need to plan and prepare. Your CV has helped you get your foot in the door; you need to do the rest!

Why is it so important to plan and prepare?

The best person for the job, in terms of the right skills, experience and achievements, doesn't always pass the interview. The best person for the job doesn't always get the job. Sometimes the most suitable candidates on paper really shoot themselves in the foot when they actually get to the interview.

The interview is one of the most critical points in the job search process. Whilst you might look great on paper, you need to be great in person. Many other factors that are not directly related to the person's ability to do the job are going to be picked up in the interview.

You've got the skills, now you need to demonstrate to the recruiter that you'll be a good fit with your future co-workers and employers. It's so easy to sabotage this valuable opportunity if you're unprepared.

On average, there are likely to be at least five other candidates being interviewed for the same vacancy. So, everything else being equal, that gives you, at the most, a 20 per cent chance of getting the job. But there's so much you can do to improve your odds of success and, in *The Interview Book*, I'll help to give you that winning edge.

What can this book do to help you?

You'll find this book useful whether you are trying to land your first job, returning to the workplace after a career break or simply looking to take another step up the career ladder. *The Interview Book* condenses the same proven methodology I use every day with my clients and contains all the tips and – dare I say it – tricks that you need. I will cut through all the debate and opinion about interviews and show you what really works from the recruiter's point of view – what I have *proved* to work.

In *The Interview Book* I will show you how to develop a winning strategy – planning and preparing for every eventuality, and learning how to handle every possible kind of interview, from a brief chat over the telephone through to a trip to an assessment centre.

I'll take you through plenty of real interview questions and make sure you know how to avoid clichés and really make an impact when handling both the classic questions and the really tough ones that interviewers can throw at you.

And I'll take you beyond the interview to discuss what you need to do to close the deal to your advantage.

Thank you for choosing *The Interview Book*. I have set out to write the most complete and up-to-date guide to interview technique on the market today; a definitive guide to interviews. I trust you will both enjoy it and find it useful. And I look forward to meeting you in cyberspace should you have any further questions. Or maybe I'll have the opportunity to coach you one-on-one myself.

I really want to help you get the job and the future you want.
Kind regards,

James Innes

James Innes
Twitter: @jamesinnes
Chairman, The CV Centre®
Author:
The CV Book
The Cover Letter Book
The Interview Book
The Interview Question & Answer Book
Ultimate New Job

Chapter **2**

Researching the job

The key to preventing pre-interview jitters is to be thoroughly prepared. We fear what we don't know and what we can't control, yet you can alleviate these fears by planning and preparing for your interview. Interviews are often seen as a gruelling experience – but they really shouldn't be.

In most cases, you will be notified that you have got through to the interview stage at least a few days in advance. You can use this time to prepare, and the better prepared you are, the fewer your reasons to be nervous.

The first item on your list should be to thoroughly research the job.

Researching the job

If you are to convince a recruiter that you are right for the role, then you need to first get it clear in your own mind why you are right for the role, and you can't do this unless you have properly researched and understood what it will involve.

Not knowing the ins and outs of a job is one of the worst blunders you can make in an interview – another is failing to demonstrate to the interviewer how you meet the requirements for the job.

A very large proportion of the questions you can expect to be asked will focus on the following two areas:

➤ Your understanding of what the job will entail, and

➤ Your suitability for fulfilling the demands of the job.

Information at your fingertips

Your first step should be to go over the job advert, description and/or person specification thoroughly. Most employers (and recruitment agencies) will have provided you with this type of information. Some organisations are kind enough to send out a whole wealth of literature to potential candidates, although most of this will relate to the organisation as a whole, not to the particular job for which you are applying. (We'll come on to researching the organisation in the next chapter.)

See how your CV compares with the employer's outline of the role, and try to identify both how and why you are a good match.

TOP TIP

• •

Compile a short list of trigger words or terms that you can refer to in the interview. This is helpful in case you freeze.

Questions you might be asked

Many interviewers will use either your CV or the job description/person specification as the agenda for your meeting. These are vital documents and you need to study them carefully. Now is the time to start envisaging what questions you might be asked – and to start drafting rough answers. We'll talk about interview questions very comprehensively later in this book but, for now, you just need to be thinking how you can demonstrate that you meet the recruiter's needs – and how you can evidence that through appropriate examples.

Questions you'd like to ask

You have the right to ask questions too. A prospective employer will not expect a candidate to make an informed decision about accepting the job if they don't have all the necessary information. Taking a list of questions with you, which you developed while researching the role, will be beneficial.

Chapter **3**

Researching the organisation

A number of popular interview questions are designed to probe and assess your knowledge of the organisation to which you are applying. An interviewer will expect you to have done your homework. If you're unprepared and unable to adequately answer these questions, then it's going to be a big black mark on your application.

Just as a lack of knowledge of the job in question will count against you, a lack of knowledge of the organisation will betray a lack of effort on your part. How can a recruiter be sure you really want this job, and that you're really the right candidate for the job if you know so little about the organisation?

BLOOPER!

· ·

A candidate, upon being asked what he could bring to the company, responded with 'What is it that you do again?'

Researching the organisation

Try to find out as much as you can about your prospective employer. The more information you have at your fingertips the better.

The Internet is an excellent research tool. Most organisations will have websites where you can read all about their history, structure, products/services etc. Some will even list biographical details of key employees, maintain archives of press releases, provide downloadable financial accounts etc. In the space of half an hour you should be able to brief yourself thoroughly.

If your prospective employer has premises that are open to the public, for example, a branch on the high street, then it may be worth your while taking the time to drop by and have a closer look. If you're applying to work for a major retail chain and you haven't even set foot inside one of its shops, then I'm sure you can see how that might be a problem. If an interviewer asks you about their shops and you have to confess you've never visited one, then it'll not only be embarrassing, it'll be extremely damaging to your chances.

Broader background research

Besides researching the organisation itself, you should also try to understand the environment in which it operates. Again, the Internet is a valuable resource, as are specialist trade journals, which can also yield a wealth of useful information.

➤ What industry or sector does the organisation operate within?

➤ How is this industry or sector currently evolving?

➤ Who are the main players within the industry or sector?

How to use this information

If you've made an effort to research both the organisation and the environment in which it operates, then you will immediately have a head start on other candidates, and you haven't even got anywhere near the interview room. Feels good, doesn't it?

Too many candidates at interview know little or nothing about the organisation they are applying to. By demonstrating that you have done at least some preliminary research into the organisation, you underline your interest, enthusiasm and motivation.

STATISTIC

Approximately 80 per cent of candidates at interview will have conducted no research whatsoever.

When planning and preparing your answers to potential interview questions, you should try to weave in little snippets of information about the organisation. Show the interviewer that you know what you're talking about. It's bound to impress them.

Being properly briefed will also help you to feel much more confident in yourself. Fear of the unknown is powerful. The more you know about your prospective employer, the less nervous you'll be when you turn up on the doorstep.

Questions to ask yourself

For your own benefit, you will also want answers to the following kinds of question:

- ➤ What does this organisation have to offer me?
- ➤ Are they the right employer for me?
- ➤ Will there be sufficient opportunities for career progression?

Thoroughly researching the organisation prior to your interview will give you the answers to some of these questions and you can fill in any blanks during the interview itself.

Chapter **4**

Mental preparation

Most of my clients are understandably nervous about attending job interviews.

We've already talked about preparing yourself on a practical basis; now it's time to talk about your mental preparation. You've got to get yourself into the right frame of mind.

Nerves

Nerves can often be a useful tool for sharpening up your performance. However, if your nerves take over to the extent that they interfere with your ability to come across professional at interview, then it's clearly a problem.

Nerves are commonly caused by your having lots of negative thoughts rattling around in your brain. Try to relax, calm your anxious mind and think positive thoughts. Remember: everyone gets nervous to some degree before an interview. It's perfectly normal.

The better prepared you are, the less likely you are to feel panicky, but you'll never completely eliminate nerves. The secret is to channel your nervous energy and use it to your advantage. Take a deep breath, focus, concentrate and don't let nerves spoil your day. In any case, most professional recruiters are trained to make allowances for the fact that you are likely to be a little on edge.

TOP TIP

Bear in mind that you always feel more nervous than you actually look. Once you realise this, you should feel a lot calmer.

Attending an interview isn't much different from going on a date, really, although in this instance, imagining them in their underwear is good for calming your nerves.

On a serious note, it's natural for you to feel threatened by an interview and for your body to be pumped full of adrenaline, and adrenaline isn't your best friend when you're trying to present yourself to the best of your ability! It might have been useful hundreds of thousands of years ago when you were cornered by a sabre-toothed tiger, but now it'll just cause you to panic even more!

Here are my top 10 key tips for calming those nerves:

➤ Stop thinking about yourself. Focus your attention on your interviewer(s).

➤ The interviewer is not your enemy!

➤ Talk to the interviewer as you would in a one-on-one conversation with anyone else, not as someone interviewing you.

➤ Ask questions to reinforce this – don't just let them ask all the questions.

➤ Have a glass of water to sip from just in case your mouth (or brain!) dries up.

➤ Take slow, deeper breaths. It'll calm you down and help get more oxygen to your brain.

➤ Smile; it's a natural relaxant, and it'll make a good impression on your interviewer too.

➤ Limit your caffeine intake; you definitely don't want to appear overly manic.

➤ Visualise the end of the interview and walking back out to freedom!

➤ Ask yourself, what's the worst that could happen; after all, it's just an interview!

Confidence

Confidence is critical to a successful interview. It is important not to go to the other extreme and appear overconfident or arrogant, which is a surprisingly common mistake. You simply need to appreciate what your strengths are and to value yourself accordingly.

Confident people inspire confidence in others; it's almost contagious. If you appear confident that you are able to do the job, the employer will be more inclined to believe that you can.

If you have been invited for interview then you obviously have something that appeals to them. Interviews are an expensive and time-consuming process and they wouldn't be making the effort unless they felt you had significant potential.

Enthusiasm

Enthusiasm in an interview is essential, but there's a fine balance. Don't overdo it! Recruiters often find that the person they are interviewing lacks enthusiasm; this will count against you. Sometimes it might just be due to nerves and shyness; don't let this happen to you. Be enthusiastic, and show it. If you're not enthusiastic about the role and about the organisation, then you won't do yourself justice. This is one of the easiest things to get right. As with confidence, enthusiasm is a trait that is guaranteed to impress an interviewer.

Show you are motivated. Talk about your work with enthusiasm. Demonstrate that you are keen to do your best.

Tone of voice

Nerves, confidence and enthusiasm will all be reflected in the way you speak. Nerves, stress and pressure will have a negative impact, whilst confidence, enthusiasm and energy will come across positively.

Take some time prior to your interview to work on your tone of voice. You might feel a little mad talking out loud to the mirror but it's an exercise that's well worth trying!

Keeping a smile on your face will also help. We'll cover that in more detail in Chapter 6: Body language.

Chapter **5**

Presentation

Presentation, presentation, presentation.

The way you physically present yourself will make an impression on the interviewer before you even open your mouth.

Image is everything! You are marketing yourself, so the way you present yourself can have an impact on the interviewer that is almost as powerful as what you actually have to say. Present yourself professionally and the interviewer will see you as a professional and vice versa.

Presentation can be the difference between success and failure.

The apparel oft proclaims the man

Yes, Shakespeare was right. Costly thy habit as thy purse can buy!

In a recent poll, the majority of recruiters cited dressing inappropriately or scruffily as the most damaging mistake a candidate can make in an interview. Candidates with bad breath or unkempt hair are also not uncommon, and often blow their chances of selection before even entering the interview room.

STATISTIC

Research has shown that your interviewer could well have made up their mind about you within 30 seconds of having met you. Use this to your advantage.

But not expressed in fancy; rich, not gaudy

I'm not going to give you any precise fashion tips; I've seen too many interview books with dodgy and often laughable fashion advice! Everyone is different; fashions change. At the end of the day it's up to you to dress as you deem appropriate.

However, here are some general guidelines I believe you should stick to. For everyone:

➤ Make sure that you have an outfit that is smart, presentable and fits you well.

➤ Clothes that can be ironed or pressed certainly should be.

➤ Clean and polish your shoes.

➤ Wash and brush your hair.

➤ Cut and file your nails.

➤ Remove any facial piercings.

➤ Unless it's really hot, you should generally keep your jacket on.

For ladies:

➤ Keep clothes plain and classic in style, avoiding fancy colours, motifs and logos.

➤ Dress conservatively – skirts shouldn't be too short; dresses shouldn't be too low-cut.

➤ Keep make-up to a sensible minimum, aiming for fresh but neutral colours.

➤ Nail polish is recommended but must be simple and freshly applied.

➤ Jewellery should be discreet.

➤ Hair clips and bands etc. should be kept to a functional minimum.

For gents:

➤ For most circumstances, you can't beat a smart, dark suit.

➤ Remain conservative in your choice of shirt colour; stick to white and shades of blue.

➤ Keep ties simple. Avoid fancy colours, motifs and logos.

➤ Get your hair cut. Short hair is generally seen as more professional than long hair.

➤ Aim for a clean-shaven look. If you have a beard or moustache, make sure it is trimmed.

➤ Limit the amount of jewellery you wear. Avoid earrings.

TOP TIP

. . . .

Try on your whole outfit before the day of the interview to check that there are no drooping hems, or buttons missing etc.

Disclaimer

The last thing I want is to cause any offence with these guidelines. You may feel you are perfectly within your rights as a man to wear an earring – and you are. However, it's probably not going to help your chances of success-fully passing an interview. My guidelines are necessarily generalised and based upon many years of experience, but it's up to your own personal judgement how you choose to present yourself.

BLOOPER!

∙∙

Some candidates wear so much perfume or aftershave that inter-viewers have been known to have to open a window!

Surf's up, dude!

Comfortable clothes will make you feel, well…comfortable. But that doesn't mean you should wear tracksuit bottoms like one candidate did. It may well be that you're hitting the beach after the interview, but it doesn't give you licence to wear flip-flops! You might think you look good in your boob tube but it sends out all the wrong signals.

Dress appropriately for the circumstances.

Your prospective employer's dress policy may be casual, but save your fashion statements until after you get the job. Dress at least as well as you would when actually turning up to do the job preferably better. Even soft-ware engineers and physicists have been known to wear suits to interviews!

Dress to impress.

If you feel that you have made an effort and look good, then you will come across as more confident and relaxed.

Lucky underwear

More than half of interview candidates admit to wearing lucky underwear to boost their confidence in an interview.

By all means, wear your lucky underwear to the interview but remem-ber that lucky underwear is not going to increase your chances of getting the job; careful preparation will. And if you take matters to extremes and believe that washing your lucky underwear will 'wear off' the luck (and, trust me, some candidates do believe this), then, depending on how little you've washed them and how often you've worn them, be warned that wearing your lucky underwear might actually count against you!

STATISTIC

· ·

A staggering 85 per cent of interview candidates take along some sort of lucky trinket, including lucky jewellery, a lucky stone, a lucky pen or even lucky shoes.

Freak accidents

Of course, there are the freak accidents like the woman who walked into an interview room with lavatory paper stuck to her shoe, or the woman who didn't notice her skirt was tucked into her knickers around the back. Then there was the man who managed to get his pants stuck in his trouser zip and had to sit through the entire interview with his pants peeking out through his fly! There's only so much you can do to avoid these sorts of things happening!

Chapter 6

Body language

The fact that you've been selected for interview means that you've made a positive impression on paper. Your next challenge is to build on this by making a positive impression in person.

Recruiters are trained to make informed assessments of candidates, based not only on how they communicate verbally but on how they communicate physically (non-verbally).

Even if your interviewer has received no formal training, they are going to be inherently sensitive to certain nuances of body language just like the rest of us. It's instinctive.

The importance of body language as a factor in the decision-making process should not be underestimated.

Positive actions

There are a number of positive actions that you can use to your advantage in an interview situation:

➤ Make and maintain eye contact without actually staring! Eye contact is essential when trying to convey trust and confidence but should not be overdone as it can come across as aggressive.

➤ Shake hands firmly but not to the extent that first aid is required! To shake someone's hand too firmly can imply arrogance and if you deliver a weak handshake it can suggest weakness. This is not just an old wives' tale – it's true. In surveys, recruiters regularly cite getting the handshake wrong as an immediate turn-off.

➤ Keep your chin up (literally and metaphorically), smile with open lips and tilt your head slightly to show that you are attentive.

➤ Place your hands with your fingertips touching together, which, believe it or not, helps to convey a sense of authority. Just don't overdo it because it's become quite a well-known technique!

Negative actions

There are an equal number of negative actions.

Some are obvious: You shouldn't pick your nails, pick your nose or any other body part for that matter!

And some are less obvious....

Here are some examples of negative traits and how they are reflected in your body language:

➤ Defensiveness: crossing your arms

➤ Boredom: feet tapping, playing with your pen, looking down, slouching

➤ Nervousness: fidgeting, thumb-twiddling, playing with your hair

➤ Arrogance/overconfidence: brisk and erect walk, hands clasped behind head

➤ Aggression: postures such as hands on hips and pointing or wagging your index finger

➤ Doubt: rubbing eyes or nose

Reading the interviewer's body language

The interviewer's body language can give you some insight into what they think about what you are saying; for example, if they're getting bored! You can then respond to that by changing the subject, for instance.

TOP TIP

An 'insider' trick is to copy certain aspects of the interviewer's body language. Imitating someone else's body language can have a positive subconscious effect on their impression of you. The theory is that they will feel that you are on the same wavelength as them and automatically become better disposed towards you. You should try to be subtle about it, and avoid copying any negative behaviour!

The importance of smiling

I'm not about to suggest you should spend the whole interview grinning like a lunatic but ... smile and the world smiles with you!

Smile at someone and the chances are that they will smile back. Try it. It's human nature; it's a built-in reflex that we have, enabling us to immediately communicate our friendly and peaceful intentions even at a distance.

It's such an innate behaviour that even if you sit by yourself and smile, you'll actually feel better for it! Again, if you don't believe me, try it!

At certain moments during your interview, a big smile is called for; particularly when you first meet and when you depart. However, you should try to keep a small smile lingering around your lips right the way through the interview, even if the going gets tough. It will definitely have a positive effect on your interviewer's perception of you (firmly proved by psychologists) and you will even feel more positive yourself.

Chapter **7**

The big day

So, The big day has finally arrived and it's soon going to be time for your interview.

Apparently, more than two-thirds of interview candidates check their horoscope for the day. If you find that reassuring then by all means do so. But try not to read too much into it, it could just end up unnerving you.

I'd suggest you concentrate your efforts on a number of other areas which I'll run through with you below.

Breakfast and lunch

Whether or not you usually have something to eat for breakfast, make an effort to have breakfast on your interview day. You might not feel much like eating (that's your nerves getting the better of you), but you definitely want to avoid going into an interview with an empty stomach. If your interview is not until the afternoon, then you should also make sure you have something to eat for lunch.

Having breakfast (or lunch) will:

➤ Boost your energy levels and help you think straight and focus.

➤ Settle any butterflies in your stomach/acid indigestion.

➤ Stops your stomach from gurgling embarrassingly!

Whilst having something to eat is definitely a good idea, it wouldn't be advisable to have too heavy a meal. That might just send you to sleep!

Setting off

Make sure that you allow yourself enough time to get ready (gather your thoughts, go to the lavatory, check your appearance in the mirror etc.).

Remember to take your letter of invitation and any documentation they have asked for, for example, photo ID or certificates.

You can't prepare for all eventualities like traffic or road accidents, so make sure you have a contact number to call in case you are going to be late.

Check the weather report. Make sure you are prepared for all possibilities. Remember: Even in summer it rains and you don't want to be soaking wet when you arrive.

Dutch courage

Avoid alcohol. If you've planned and prepared properly you won't need any 'Dutch courage'. There are numerous stories of shy or nervous candidates turning up at interview after one drink too many, including a bus driver!

Not only does alcohol impair your judgement, the interviewer will probably smell it on you.

It's probably best to avoid drinking too much the night before as well. You don't want to turn up for an interview hungover and dehydrated, and suffer from the dreaded 'dry mouth'. It could make it rather difficult to answer the questions!

Conversely, you should also avoid drinking too much water because you certainly don't want to have to interrupt the interview to go to the lavatory. Going to the lavatory on arrival for your interview or just prior to your departure never makes for a very good impression either.

It's now been fairly conclusively proved that drinking coffee doesn't actually cause dehydration. However, limiting your caffeine intake is advisable nonetheless. You definitely don't want to appear overly manic to your interviewer. If you've ever seen the film *Trainspotting*, then you may recall Spud's famous interview! If not then try searching for 'Spud trainspotting interview video' on the Internet and you'll be sure to find a clip.

You should also avoid any non-prescription drugs.

BLOOPER!

Asked if he would mind undergoing a drugs test, one candidate replied, 'Not at all – I'm happy to test any drugs you like!'

TOP TIP

You should always make sure you take a copy of your CV – or application form – with you so that you can refer to it immediately prior to – and even during – the interview if necessary. Ideally you shouldn't need to refer to it too much; reading through it shortly before the interview should be sufficient to refresh your memory of its contents.

Interview with a vampire

I would recommend steering clear of garlic, curry and other pungent foods before your interview, or even the night before. They're likely to remain on your breath and, if you sweat when you're nervous (and most of us do), the organic chemicals that cause these odours are likely to ooze out of your skin and evaporate into the air around you. Best avoided, really!

Also, whilst you might feel a greater need for a cigarette than usual, try a nicotine patch for the day instead. Smoke before an interview and the smell will follow you into the interview room on your breath, your clothes and in your hair. As an ex-smoker myself, I know that nicotine patches don't relieve the craving as effectively as a cigarette does but today is definitely one day when it will be worth the suffering!

Gum chum

Whilst chewing gum might be a good idea to freshen your breath before your interview, make sure you discard it before you arrive for the interview. I have interviewed candidates who chewed their way through an interview, and it definitely doesn't make for a good impression. Neither does it make for a good impression to arrive in reception and drop your gum in the bin. Bin it before you even get to the premises.

HELLO?! YES! NO! I'M AT AN INTERVIEW! WHAT?!

Surveys show that having a mobile phone ring during an interview, or worse, actually answering a mobile phone during an interview, is a top ten reason for a recruiter to reject a candidate. Unless you're applying to work as a Dom Joly lookalike, don't even think about leaving your phone switched on.

➤ Make sure your mobile phone is switched off before you get to the interview.

➤ Make sure it stays switched off during the interview.

➤ Make sure it stays switched off until you have most definitely left the building.

➤ Make sure you don't forget any of the above!

BLOOPER!

One candidate answered her phone and then asked if the interviewer would mind leaving his own office because it was a 'private' conversation!

If you do forget to turn your phone off and it rings during the interview, ignore it, or turn it off as discreetly as possible so as to ensure it doesn't ring again, and apologise sincerely to the interviewer. You might just about be able to salvage the situation.

Chapter **8**

First impressions count

How quickly do you sum up someone you've just met? It's probably less than a couple of minutes.

First impressions are extremely important. Interviewers can reach a decision about a candidate very quickly, so make sure you walk into the room as if you really want the job. Make a poor first impression and you might not be able to recover from it.

Remember: you never get a second chance to make a first impression!

Taking centre stage

You are on show from the moment you arrive at your employer's premises. Your interview starts immediately. Walk confidently into the building, smile at the receptionist, introduce yourself and explain who it is that you've come to see and why. Try not to look like you've just arrived for your own execution!

TOP TIP

Always be polite and friendly with reception staff; they can have a surprising amount of influence in an organisation, not least because they know absolutely everyone.

In the waiting room

You will more than likely be asked to take a seat and wait for a few minutes whilst someone comes to meet you.

There are those who say that you shouldn't sit and that you should remain standing because this somehow conveys enthusiasm. I don't quite grasp that personally, research into body language reveals that most people perceive a sitting position as conveying confidence, power and authority. I feel your time is better spent sitting down, trying to relax and compose yourself. It probably wouldn't hurt to pick up any corporate literature that happens to be lying around and read it, or at least pretend to be reading, with interest. It may in fact help to get you in the right frame of mind.

First contact

The most likely person to come and collect you is the interviewer themselves. However, don't count on it. An assistant could easily be sent. Regardless, you should stand up the moment you are approached, move forward to greet them, smile and deliver a decent handshake. They will introduce themselves and you will then know who you are dealing with. No matter who it is, as with the reception staff, be polite and friendly.

Small talk

On the way to the interview/meeting room it is normal to engage in a bit of light chat as to your health, your journey, the weather, the news headlines, the sorts of things we Brits normally chat about to fill in awkward silences! An interviewer is much more likely to look favourably on a candidate with whom they feel they have developed a rapport, so try to be friendly without being overly familiar. Don't babble and speak clearly; mumbling can be judged the same way as a weak handshake.

Places, please!

As you enter the interview room you will be invited to sit down. Take your seat, sit up straight and face the interviewer as if you are almost eager for the first question to be asked!

Final impressions matter too

At the end of the interview you will normally be escorted to the exit. Give the interviewer a final handshake, smile and leave with your head held high.

You were on show from the moment you arrived and you remain on show until you are out of sight. If the stress of it was all too much for you, don't get your fags out of your pocket and light up the moment you're out the door. And if you think you've done well, don't perform a victory dance on the pavement, and avoid screeching excitedly at someone on your mobile phone. Basically, don't do anything except get yourself away and out of sight as quickly and quietly as possible!

PART **2**

INTERVIEW SCENARIOS: EXPECT THE UNEXPECTED

Chapter **9**

Basic principles

Interviews vary enormously. Most people's conception of an interview is a classic one-on-one interview, which is what most candidates may well be expecting; however, there are a multitude of possible scenarios.

> ➤ Classic one-on-one interviews
> ➤ Panel interviews
> ➤ Competency based interviews
> ➤ Psychometric and aptitude tests
> ➤ Presentations
> ➤ Group interviews
> ➤ Assessment centres
> ➤ Distance interviews

The interview may be a quick, informal chat across a crowded office or it could involve a panel of interviewers all firing questions at you. You may be asked to sit an aptitude test or prove that you have the necessary skills for the job, a typing test, for example. There may even be group activities with other candidates, designed to see how you perform in a team situation.

Often, candidates fail to perform to the best of their abilities because they were thrown into a situation they were not expecting.

My advice?

You can't prepare for every eventuality, but you can certainly prepare for most, and in the following chapters I will cover all the most likely scenarios.

Second and third interviews

Generally, you will only be expected to attend one interview. However, it is important for you to be aware that many employers will require a second interview, or even a third.

The advice in this book applies equally to all interviews whether your first, second or third – the basic principles remain the same.

You shouldn't necessarily expect that each of the interviews will be of the same type, though. Your first interview might be by telephone, followed by a panel interview and ending with an assessment centre for your third interview. Regardless of the scenario, second and third interviews are generally more intensive and detailed.

There's nothing to worry about, though. If you've planned and prepared for all the following possible interview scenarios, then you should be able to sail through the process, no matter how many interviews you are subjected to.

You should also find that the first interview gives you some idea of what to expect in your second or third interviews, enabling you to be fully prepared.

Chapter **10**

Classic one-on-one interviews

Mano a mano

Swords at dawn

Many candidates, faced with a one-on-one interview, get the feeling they are taking part in a duel!

Thinking all the power lies with the interviewer is a misguided belief.

You should always remember that an interview is a two-way process of recruiter and candidate learning more about each other. It's just as much about whether or not they will make a suitable employer as whether or not you will make a suitable employee.

Dealing with different interviewers

Interviewers vary widely in their level of experience, from highly qualified HR professionals all the way down to someone conducting their very first interview. A friend of mine was once interviewed for a position by someone who clearly had never conducted an interview in his life – and she ended up having to turn the tables and lead the interview herself!

Friendly but professionally detached

In any one-on-one situation it's important to establish a rapport with your interviewer. An interview should be a friendly, professional discussion. You might not enjoy the experience; the other person might not enjoy the experience, but the more enjoyable you can make it, the better the outcome.

Whilst rapport is important, being too intimate or matey with the interviewer is definitely to be avoided. You need to keep a certain professional distance.

Many people instinctively try to be humorous in order to break the ice in tense or awkward situations but jokes are generally out of place at interviews.

BLOOPER!

• •

The candidate who said he smoked weed when asked what he did in his spare time and the candidate who said that a threesome was his greatest achievement most probably thought they were building rapport with the interviewer by being witty and amusing. But did it get them the job? No!

The importance of mock interviews

Undertaking mock interviews with someone you trust is probably the best way to practise your interview technique, apart from sitting through a number of real interviews.

Ask someone to sit down with you for 30 minutes or so and ask you some of the questions we'll be covering later in this book.

It's all very well to sit down by yourself and write out perfect answers to all the common questions but it's certainly not the same as having a real live human being sit opposite you and ask you the questions face-to-face.

Chapter **11**

Panel interviews

A panel interview is an extension of the one-on-one interview with more interviewers present at the meeting.

In my experience candidates are considerably more nervous about attending a panel interview than they would be if they were attending a one-on-one interview. However, there's really no need to be.

In this chapter I'll cover the few points you need to bear in mind when attending a panel interview and you'll see that there's really nothing to worry about.

Because two, three or more heads are better than one, you can definitely expect your panel interview to be quite intense, but provided you've prepared thoroughly, there shouldn't be anything you can't cope with.

The panel

The first step is to identify who is on the panel and what role each person is fulfilling – why are they there? Panel members won't expect you to be telepathic; they'll be polite and introduce themselves and you should be able to easily deduce the reason for each person's presence.

A panel will always have a 'chair', a person who is ostensibly in charge of proceedings and who will be responsible for guiding the overall direction of the interview. They will normally be easy to identify as they have a tendency to sit either in the middle of the other interviewers or on their own at the head of the table.

TOP TIP

If you're attending a panel interview take several copies of your CV with you. It's very common to find poorly prepared interviewers sharing a copy and if you've brought along extra copies for them then it's bound to impress.

The chair will be assisted in questioning you by the other panel members. Panel interviews are popular where it is not considered practical for one single person to effectively assess your suitability for a role. A typical three-person panel could, for example, consist of a department manager acting as chair, assisted by your prospective line manager and perhaps a prospective colleague to question you on specific technical issues.

Eyes on the prize

In a one-on-one interview it's simple enough to make an appropriate amount of eye contact with your interviewer. However, in a panel interview you must make an effort to make regular eye contact with all panel members in reasonably equal measure. You must build rapport with each and every one of them. Easier said than done, but eye contact is an excellent start.

You talkin' to me?

Also, in a one-on-one interview there's only one person to whom to give your answers. In a panel interview, when one panel member poses a question, focus attentively on that individual but, when it comes to answering, you must address your answer to all of the panel members.

Don't allow your eyes to flit backwards and forth like a rabbit caught in the headlights. As you start your answer, focus on the panel member who asked you the question but, as you make your points, steer your gaze steadily from one panel member to another – in no particular order. If you're experienced in giving presentations then you'll be familiar with this technique. (I'll talk in detail about presentations in Chapter 14: Presentations.)

Avoid focusing too much of your attention on just one panel member, for example, the chair or the person who asks the majority of the questions. All panel members will contribute to reaching a decision on your application, and a quieter, less prominent panel member could easily have a surprising amount of influence. Treat them all as equals.

Time to go

When your interview draws to a close, ensure that you smile and thank each of the panel members. Given that it is most likely the chair that will wrap up the interview and indicate to you that the interview is over, it's a natural reaction to only thank the chair. Avoid this mistake and make one final positive impression on all the interviewers. As I say, you really don't know which one will have the casting vote on your appointment to the role.

Chapter **12**

Competency-based, behavioural and situational interviews

There's a lot of talk about competency-based interviews, behavioural interviews and questioning, situational interviews, evidence-based interviewing etc. They're all the rage.

It is possible you've heard of these concepts but aren't sure what they actually mean.

What is a competency?

The first issue to address is what is actually meant by the word 'competency'. If you look in a dictionary it will tell you that the word 'competence' means 'the condition of being capable; ability'. The word 'competency' is derived from this.

Competency-based interviewing, therefore, focuses on analysing your ability to handle certain specific tasks and situations, drawing on a combination of your skills and your experience. By examining in detail your past performance, an interviewer will be aiming to effectively judge your future potential to fulfil the role for which you are now applying. It helps the interviewer to answer the following two key questions:

➤ Can you do the job?

➤ Do you have what it takes?

Competency-based questions

Competency-based questions can take a wide variety of different formats and approaches. Many of the questions I cover later in this book probe and analyse key competencies.

➤ Can you tell me about a major problem at work that you've had to deal with?

➤ What techniques do you use to get things done?

➤ Can you tell me about a time when you have failed to achieve a goal?

➤ Are you able to make difficult decisions and tough choices?

➤ Can you tell me about a major project you have successfully completed?

➤ How did you cope with the most difficult colleague you've ever had?

➤ Can you give me an example of when you have successfully coached a member of your team?

These sorts of questions enable interviewers to identify qualities and attributes such as:

➤ Analytical skills
➤ Problem solving
➤ Creativity
➤ Communication
➤ Planning and organisation
➤ Self-development
➤ Motivation
➤ Objectivity
➤ Management
➤ Integrity

Situational interview questions

In contrast to the competency-based interviews that ask you to reflect on past experiences, situational interviews require you to explain how you would deal with a specific situation if it arose in the future. Again, interviewers are looking to establish if you have what it takes to do the job, but you will not have the luxury of being able to refer to past experiences so these can be more complicated.

Questions in a situational interview are designed to assess how you would handle hypothetical problems without the advantage of preparation. So whilst you do not necessarily refer directly to past experiences in a situational interview, you can certainly learn from them. Think back to problems you have dealt with successfully in the past, recall what action you took and relate this to the hypothetical situation you are presented with.

Examples of situational interview questions include:

➤ What would you do if the priorities on a project you were working on changed suddenly?
➤ How would you deal with a customer who is unhappy with the service they have received?
➤ What would you do if the work of a subordinate or team member was not up to expectations?
➤ You disagree with the way your supervisor tells you to handle a problem. What would you do?

➤ How would you handle a difficult colleague who is lowering morale within the team?

➤ Describe how you would handle the situation if you met resistance when introducing a new idea or policy to a team or work group.

➤ How would you handle it if you believed strongly in a recommendation you made in a meeting, but most of your colleagues strongly disagreed?

➤ Can you describe a group situation where you were the only person who disagreed with a point of view or action? How did you handle it? What were the results?

➤ Tell me about a time when you had to stick by a decision you made even though it made you unpopular.

➤ Describe a situation where you needed to work with a client or customer who was very different from you.

Answering competency-based questions

You will find lots more specifics in the next few chapters, but there are some important guidelines to consider first when answering competency-based questions. In particular, I need to emphasise the importance of using examples from your own experience to illustrate your answers.

Some questions will specifically demand an example, e.g. 'Can you give me an example of when you have successfully coached a member of your team?' Others won't ask for an example but you'll be expected to give one anyway if your answer is to have any validity, e.g. 'Are you able to make difficult decisions and tough choices?'

The interviewer is looking for you to tell a brief story describing the situation, explaining your behaviour and highlighting the benefits of your actions. It's no good just saying you possess certain abilities; you need to prove it by outlining how you have demonstrated the behaviour. Competency-based questions quickly expose fakes.

Experiences from the workplace, including voluntary work, are generally considered to be much stronger than examples from your studies, hobbies or personal life. But as long as the example you give covers the competence in question, it will still be appropriate.

Examples of situations with positive outcomes are also considered to have more impact than ones with a negative outcome; naturally you want the interview to see you in the best light. If, however, you are required to use a more negative example, i.e. a project that was not delivered on time, then you just need to make sure that your answer demonstrates what you have learned from this particular situation and that you know what you would do differently next time.

The STAR technique

When preparing possible answers to competency-based questions, the STAR technique is a really useful way of ensuring that you give examples that emphasise the contribution that you made and what the outcome was whilst keeping your response concise.

Here is a breakdown of the STAR structure:

S = Situation (set the context with a brief outline of the example you are using)

T = Task (what was specifically required of you, not other people in the team)

A = Action (what activities you engaged in/what you actually did)

R = Result (what the outcome was of your contribution to this specific situation – ideally this will be a positive outcome but if the outcome was negative, you will need to describe what you have learnt from it)

Key to the successful use of the STAR technique is making sure that your personal contribution and actions are clearly articulated at each stage of the process. It is also important not to make it obvious to the interviewer that you have used this technique! Make your answers flow seamlessly.

Identifying required competencies

Competency-based interviewing is now such an integral part of most interviews that, apart from defining it in this chapter, I haven't treated it separately within this book. I have scattered examples of competency-based questions throughout my lists of the most popular interview questions.

However, my examples are necessarily generalised. In order to prepare properly for your interviews, you will need to identify the specific competencies your prospective employer requires. This applies to both competency-based and situational interviews.

Back in Chapter 2: Researching the job, I emphasised how important it is to thoroughly study any job description or person specification you have. This should enable you to identify most, if not all, of the key competencies for which an interviewer is going to be seeking evidence. And you should try to establish the perfect example (preferably more than one example) for each and every one of their criteria.

Follow-up questions

Whilst you should always endeavour to answer each question comprehensively, you can expect a skilled interviewer to hit you with a number of follow-up questions. There are only a certain number of different competencies required for the average job and your interviewer is going to want to question you very thoroughly on each one. But if you've carefully prepared and thought through your examples in advance, then their follow-up questions should be easy enough to tackle.

TOP TIP

They will be looking for weaknesses in your answers and flaws in your arguments, so stay on the ball, concentrate and be careful you're not tripped up.

A level playing field

Whilst competency-based questions can – and will – crop up in almost any interview, some employers will have a very formal policy of competency-based interviewing. It's an increasingly popular technique.

This usually means that they will establish in advance what the key competencies are that they are looking for, and they will design a series of questions to help them determine which candidates are best able to fulfil these. In such interviews, all candidates will normally be asked exactly the same set of questions in the same sequence (often with a variety of follow-up questions). It's considered to be one of the fairest – and most thorough – selection techniques available.

Whenever you hear someone referring to a competency-based interview, this is generally what they mean.

Not so complicated after all, is it?

Chapter **13**

Psychometric and aptitude tests

Most readers will be familiar with the idea of psychometric and aptitude tests, even if you haven't necessarily been subjected to one yet. In this chapter I'm going to give you a brief outline of the various different types of test an employer is likely to roll out. These types of tests are surprisingly common – and their popularity is on the increase. Indeed, The CV Centre® has recently introduced aptitude testing as a way of helping us to shortlist when recruiting.

STATISTIC

Over 75 per cent of FTSE 100 companies use some form of psycho-metric or aptitude testing in their recruitment processes.

Chances are you will experience one test or another during your career, and for the unprepared candidate such tests can present significant chal-lenges. So it is important to have an idea of what to expect.

The main types of psychometric and aptitude (also known as 'ability') tests I'll be talking about are:

➤ Personality tests/questionnaires

➤ Verbal reasoning

➤ Numeracy/numerical reasoning

➤ Spatial and diagrammatic reasoning

➤ Clerical and data checking

General tips

Most tests will be delivered under 'exam conditions', with a specific time limit set for their completion. I'm not saying you should rush though; keeping your cool and avoiding silly mistakes are essential. And if you manage your time to allow for checking of your work at the end you will probably do better than if you go very slowly, as you will then probably be better able to go back and focus on questions you were unsure of.

As in any exam, carefully observe any instructions you are given and, most importantly, make sure that you read each question carefully!

EXAMPLE

You have 10 minutes for this test, which consists of 8 questions.

1 I always enjoy meeting new people.
   (a) True
   (b) False

2 I am always methodical and organised when meeting a deadline.
   (a) True
   (b) False
   (c) Can't say

3 I like to check my work in detail.
   (a) True
   (b) In between
   (c) False

4 I don't suffer fools gladly.
   (a) Strongly agree
   (b) Agree
   (c) Neither agree nor disagree
   (d) Disagree
   (e) Strongly disagree

5 If I go to a party I...
   (a) get into the spirit of things quickly and am often the centre of attention.
   (b) tend to look for any familiar faces and start talking to someone I know.
   (c) stand in a quiet corner and observe things for a while.
   (d) approach someone who looks shy and start talking to them.

6 Which of these two statements describes the way you more usually think or feel?
   (a) You find it easy to keep a conversation going in almost any situation.
   (b) You find it easy to keep a conversation going only with people you know well.

7 Do you usually get on well with people who are:
   (a) full of common sense?
   (b) imaginative?

8 From the alternatives given below choose the one that describes you most and the one that describes you least.
   (a) I like to relax with friends.
   (b) I prefer to spend my spare time alone.
   (c) Some people see me as reserved.
   (d) I like to make work fun.

Personality tests/questionnaires

A personality test is normally a series of multiple-choice questions, which assess you on how you respond to – or feel about – a given situation. They're carefully designed so that you can't 'game' them, i.e. identify which of the responses is 'right' – and you shouldn't see such tests in terms of right and wrong anyway. Everybody has a different personality. The employer simply wants to gain some deeper insight into your own personality – the goal being to judge how close a match you are to the needs of the role for which you are applying. My advice is to always answer all questions as truthfully as possible.

Verbal reasoning

Verbal reasoning tests are designed to assess how well your brain handles, understands, processes, analyses and interprets language. They will include questions testing your spelling and grammar, as well as questions which identify whether you can spot synonyms, antonyms, analogies etc.

EXAMPLE

You have 5 minutes for this test, which consists of 10 questions.
   Answers can be found at the end of this chapter.
   For the following words, choose the one from the alternatives given that is closest to it in meaning.

   1 dogged
      (a) determined
      (b) lazy
      (c) tenacious
      (d) ruthless
   2 impudent
      (a) cute
      (b) cheeky
      (c) reckless
      (d) childish
   3 porcelain
      (a) china
      (b) crockery
      (c) earthenware
      (d) tea service

For each of the following words, choose the one from the alternatives given that is most nearly opposite to it in meaning.

4 giant
   (a) large
   (b) pygmy
   (c) elf
   (d) troll
5 dear
   (a) beloved
   (b) elk
   (c) cheap
   (d) costly
6 quickly
   (a) rapidly
   (b) urgently
   (c) lazily
   (d) slowly

Choose the word from the alternatives given that best fits the gap in each sentence.

7 Ted was small, but very noisy and chatty, so he made his .... felt.
   (a) opinions
   (b) presence
   (c) voice
   (d) conversation
8 Had it not been for the .... arrival of reinforcements the battle would have been lost.
   (a) general's
   (b) late
   (c) timely
   (d) urgent
9 Martha gave her grandson a .... when he passed his exams.
   (a) smile
   (b) present
   (c) certificate
   (d) telling-off
10 I am going to the match too, so would you like a .... in my car?
   (a) seat
   (b) trip
   (c) lift
   (d) journey

Numeracy/Numerical reasoning

Numerical reasoning tests are the numerical equivalent of verbal reasoning tests. You're not expected to have studied mathematics to a high level; the concepts involved are all relatively simple and certainly shouldn't require a calculator. You will be expected to perform simple mental calculations and identify patterns and sequences. Other questions may give you a graph or chart and probe your understanding of it.

EXAMPLE

You have 5 minutes for this test, which consists of 8 questions.
Answers can be found at the end of this chapter.
Select the correct answer from the alternatives given.

1 83 – 17
   (a) 66
   (b) 47
   (c) 56
   (d) 100
2 242 ÷ 11
   (a) 32
   (b) 22
   (c) 31
   (d) 42
3 1.8 – 7.2
   (a) 9
   (b) 54
   (c) –5.4
   (d) –5.6
4 How many 30 centilitre bottles can be completely filled from a 100 litre container?
   (a) 300
   (b) 3,000
   (c) 330
   (d) 333

5 What number comes next in the series 2, 4, 8, 32, 256?
   (a) 512
   (b) 820
   (c) 8,192
   (d) 524,288

6 What number is missing from the series 1, 8, 512, 4,096?
   (a) 2
   (b) 129
   (c) 128
   (d) 64

7 Rounded up to the nearest whole number, what is the average speed of a barge which travels 3 km in half an hour and 2 km in the next quarter of an hour?
   (a) 5 kph
   (b) 6 kph
   (c) 7 kph
   (d) 4 kph

8 If a passenger tells a taxi driver to keep the change when they give them a £20 note for a fare of £18.36, what is their tip as a percentage of that £20?
   (a) 10.1%
   (b) 8.9%
   (c) 8.0%
   (d) 8.2%

Spatial and diagrammatic reasoning

Spatial and diagrammatic reasoning is classic IQ test territory. You will be shown a variety of different shapes and patterns, and be expected to identify differences, commonalities and/or deduce matching members of a set. Questions frequently include 3D images represented in 2D and are designed to test how able you are to visualise an image (to project the image in your mind's eye) and to then manipulate that image. On a more practical level, questions could test your ability to follow a map or street plan.

EXAMPLE

You have 5 minutes for this test, which consists of 5 questions.

Answers can be found at the end of this chapter.

For each of the following questions, choose the pattern from the list of alternatives, a–d, which continues the sequence in the line above.

For each of the following questions, choose the alternative, a–d, which fits in with the set in the line above.

These questions are reproduced from Edenborough (2009): *Brilliant Psychometric Tests*, Prentice Hall, © Pearson Education Limited 2009.

Clerical and data checking

You are naturally most likely to encounter these sorts of test if you are applying for clerical or data entry/control positions. The principle behind them is that they measure accuracy since this is clearly a very important consideration in such roles, from taking down a phone number to entering product codes on order forms. You will not be faced with complexity in such tests, just a series of similar, quite simple, questions.

EXAMPLE

You have 5 minutes for this test, which consists of 10 questions.

Answers can be found at the end of this chapter.

Read the following passage and answer the questions which follow it.

X-Ray Airlines have just taken over their rival, Hainault Skyways. The routes are not being changed yet, but many of the flight numbers are being changed. All of the X-Ray numbers below 381 are to be changed so that the first digit is now 7, but otherwise unaltered, and all of the Hainault numbers are to be changed to X-Ray numbers, applying the same rule to numbers below 381. Indicate which of the flight numbers in the following chart have been correctly and which incorrectly changed.

	Old	New
1	XR297	XR797
2	HS481	XR781
3	XR442	XR442
4	XR552	HS552
5	HS228	XR728
6	HS403	XR403
7	XR242	XR742
8	HS181	XR181
9	XR555	XR555
10	XR382	XR782

1	(a) right	(b) wrong
2	(a) right	(b) wrong
3	(a) right	(b) wrong
4	(a) right	(b) wrong
5	(a) right	(b) wrong
6	(a) right	(b) wrong
7	(a) right	(b) wrong
8	(a) right	(b) wrong
9	(a) right	(b) wrong
10	(a) right	(b) wrong

Getting in some practice

As you can see from the examples in the previous pages, the best way to prepare for psychometric and aptitude tests is to actually practise them. The CV Centre® has put together a set of free online tools which will help you to get some practice on all these different types of test. Please visit: **www.jamesinn.es**

Further reading

Psychometric and aptitude testing is a popular subject that goes way beyond the scope of this book. All of the examples above are excerpts from four different books which I'd strongly recommend you read if you would like to learn more about these sorts of test.

> *Brilliant Psychometric Tests*
> *Brilliant Tactics to Pass Aptitude Tests*
> *Brilliant Numeracy Tests*
> *Brilliant Verbal Reasoning Tests*

You can order copies via our website: **www.jamesinn.es**

Answers to the example tests

EXAMPLE	Verbal reasoning
1 c	
2 b	
3 a	
4 b	
5 c	
6 d	
7 b	
8 c	
9 b	
10 c	

EXAMPLE	Numeracy/Numerical reasoning

1 (a) 66
2 (b) 22
3 (c) −5.4
4 (d) 333
5 (c) 8,192
6 (d) 64
7 (c) 7 kph
8 (d) 8.2%

EXAMPLE	Spatial and diagrammatic reasoning

1 (d) The shapes move clockwise and alternate between L and ⌐.
2 (a) The sequence moves progressively from left to right.
3 (a) There are six shapes each time, drawn from the same set. One or more of those might appear twice or more each time.
4 (c) There are three shapes in each top line, a square in the second or third line and a triangle in the fourth line.
5 (b) There are two ⊣ shapes and two ⊤ shapes, which may be rotated in each case.

EXAMPLE	Clerical and data checking

1 a
2 b
3 a
4 b
5 a
6 a
7 a
8 b
9 a
10 b

Chapter **14**

Presentations

In many lines of work, the ability to give powerful presentations is a key skill. As a consequence, it is very common for organisations to request that candidates prepare a brief presentation for delivery at their interview. It's an excellent opportunity to demonstrate your ability to organise yourself, plan, prepare and communicate effectively, so you'd better make sure you get it right.

Preparation

In most circumstances, an employer will be decent enough to warn you that you'll be expected to give a presentation, giving you plenty of time to carry out any necessary research, write, memorise and practise your presentation.

TOP TIP

Make sure your presentation follows a clear and logical structure, beginning with a suitable introduction and closing with an appropriate conclusion. It's always the beginning and the ending of a presentation that get the most attention.

Usually, you will be given a specific topic for the presentation as well as a suggested length. It is essential you adhere to any such guidelines.

A recruiter may really put you to the test by surprising you on the day with an invitation to give a presentation. In this situation, you can only really be expected to deliver a presentation on a topic you're familiar with, so pre-empt this and, if giving presentations forms part of your job description, have a brief presentation ready regardless of whether or not you've been specifically asked to do so.

Delivery

Nerves are probably the biggest enemy you face when delivering a presentation. You're up there at the front all alone with everyone staring at you! It's a natural instinct for you to feel threatened by this. However, bear in mind that members of the audience are (normally!) on your side and that they are not your enemy – your nerves are. Don't let your nerves win the battle because it'll reflect immediately in your tone of voice.

TOP TIP

Speak confidently. Slightly slower, slightly louder and slightly more deeply than you would normally do, and articulate each syllable clearly.

Cue cards

Many presenters, me included, rely on cue cards to help them through their presentation.

Reading from a script is totally unacceptable and, whilst you should make an effort to memorise as much of your presentation as possible, memorising it verbatim is likely to result in a fairly stiff and stilted delivery.

By using cue cards you can identify the next point you wish to make with a quick downward glance, helping you to spend most of your time maintaining eye contact with your audience.

Eye contact

Eye contact is essential to effective communication. If you've got an audience in front of you then don't focus too much on any one person; move your gaze randomly around the room and aim to make brief eye contact with everyone. Once you've established eye contact, they're a lot more likely to listen to what you have to say. You may even find that they nod their head in agreement!

Physical gestures

Whilst it's normally fine to walk up and down a little bit, you should avoid pacing the floor excessively. Likewise, it's fine to gesture with your hands, but try to keep it within reasonable limits. You want to convey the impression of someone who is calm and in control – even if you do have a swarm of butterflies in your stomach!

Visual aids

You should be notified in advance whether or not you are expected to use any visual aids; for example, a PowerPoint slideshow. If it's not specified then there's nothing to be lost in asking – a PowerPoint presentation is always more powerful than a straightforward verbal presentation. It also gives you an opportunity to demonstrate your proficiency with PowerPoint.

Practice makes perfect

The secret to a successful presentation is practice. Practise reciting your presentation by yourself, practise in front of the mirror and practise in front of a friend.

The more you practise your presentation, the more confident you will become.

Q&A

As you finish your presentation, it will be expected that you ask members of your audience whether they have any questions. You should endeavour to anticipate the type of questions you are likely to be asked and have prepared rough answers in advance.

Finally, it's always a nice touch to thank your audience for listening.

Chapter **15**

Group interviews

A group interview is defined as one in which multiple candidates attend and are assessed simultaneously. The candidates not only get to meet each other but are actually expected to work together on a variety of different tasks, whilst being carefully observed and having their behaviour noted in detail.

Why a group interview?

What are the employer's motivations in interviewing candidates in a group context rather than one on one? It could be a time-saving exercise or it could be because they place above-average importance on teamwork – or it could be both. Whatever you think their motivations, you should assume that the organisation is looking to identify how you work within a team – what role you naturally fulfil.

What role do you fulfil?

Look at it this way: what role do they want you to fulfil?

Are they looking for a leader? Are they looking for someone who brings out the best in others? Are they looking for the person who generates the ideas or the person who is a dab hand at putting new ideas into practice?

Establish in your own mind what sort of a team player they want you to be and it will help to guide your behaviour.

Maybe you are applying for a role as a team leader. This doesn't mean that you have to be utterly overbearing and demonstrate to everyone, at all costs, that you're the boss. Is the employer looking for a fascist dictator? The loudest, brashest, pushiest candidate is rarely the one selected.

You can demonstrate that you work well within a group without aggressively taking the lead.

Working well within a group means listening, cooperating, communicating, generating ideas and solutions. Do you help the group to achieve its objectives or are you more of a hindrance?

Group activities

There are two main types of activity you are likely to encounter at a group interview:

➤ Verbal activities
➤ Physical activities.

In a verbal group interview, the group will typically be given a topic (or topics) to discuss, debate and reach a conclusion on. A chair may be appointed by the interviewer (or the interviewer may themselves chair the discussion) or you may all be expected to contribute equally.

Alternatively, you could be assigned role-play exercises; working in small groups of two or more to act out carefully designed scenarios, which could be related to the job on offer or could be of a more abstract, psychological nature.

It's also a popular technique to ask each candidate to give a brief presentation to the other candidates. Please refer back to the previous chapter for detailed advice on how to handle presentations.

In a physical group interview, activities can vary widely. You may be expected to plan, design and/or physically construct something, or solve a problem or puzzle. Expect the unexpected.

The other candidates

You're going to be spending a few hours – maybe a whole day – with other candidates. Whilst you might, quite reasonably, see them as competition, there's no reason to treat them as enemies. On the contrary, you will be assessed on your ability to get on with and to work with these people, so aim to be friendly and communicative right from the start. Make friends, not enemies. Remember that you're a team.

TOP TIP

Don't be so loud that you drown everyone else out. Conversely, don't be so quiet that nobody even notices you!

Under the spotlight

You will be closely observed throughout the day. That might sound stressful but try to keep calm – everyone is in the same boat and they're probably all just as nervous as you.

Key factors on which you will be assessed include communication, initiative, motivation, determination and the ability to function effectively under pressure.

From the moment you arrive to the moment you leave you'll be under the spotlight.

Chapter **16**

Distance interviews

There's no rule that says you have to attend in person for an interview.

Telephone interviews have been commonplace for decades. With the advent of technologies such as video-conferencing and the Internet, an employer at one end of the country can now easily and immediately interview a potential employee at the other end.

I call such interviews 'distance' interviews and in this chapter we'll look at how you should handle them.

Telephone interviews

Telephone interviews are most commonly used as a shortlisting technique, to whittle down a large number of applicants to a final shortlist that will be called in for face-to-face interviews. As such, they are more commonly used for first interviews, rather than second or third interviews. However, if you are widely geographically separated from your interviewer then it may be more convenient to conduct the entire process by telephone. It all depends on the employer.

A telephone interview is similar to a one-on-one interview. The main difference is that you won't, of course, have any visual cues – and neither will they. Issues such as dress sense and body language are immediately irrelevant but most of my other interview advice still applies.

In particular, you need to concentrate on articulating clearly and getting your tone of voice right. The interviewer might not be able to see you smiling but they will be able to hear it in your voice – and they'll also be able to hear a frown!

BLOOPER!

When I was very much younger, I allowed myself to be interviewed by telephone with my rather rude African Grey parrot within earshot! And one indignant interviewer reported to a survey that he once had a candidate flush the lavatory on him during a telephone interview!

Do be careful of background noises and try to conduct the interview somewhere calm and quiet, rather than on a busy street corner! You should especially avoid eating, drinking, smoking or chewing gum during the interview, as all of these will be distinctly audible. The only exception to this would be for you to take an occasional sip of water to stop your mouth drying up.

Whilst there's nothing wrong with taking a copy of your CV (or application form) or other notes into any interview, a telephone interview makes this much easier. You can lay out all your papers neatly in front of you, so you can put your finger on the precise document you need at a moment's notice.

➤ CV or application form

➤ Job advert, description or person specification

➤ A list of the key selling points you want to make

➤ A list of the questions you would like to ask

➤ Diary or calendar to schedule a follow-up interview

Whilst it's always better if the interviewer doesn't know that you're referring to notes, it is much more socially acceptable to refer to papers when you are on the phone than when you are sitting face to face in a formal interview setting.

TOP TIP

It will also be much easier for you to take notes yourself – especially if you have a hands-free or loudspeaker facility on your telephone. By taking brief notes as you go along, you can rely on them later when attending a second or third interview – or even use them to help prepare yourself for other interviews.

If the interviewer has arranged to call you:

➤ Ensure you provide them with the correct telephone number.

➤ Ensure you are fully prepared and ready to answer at the designated time.

➤ Ensure that nobody else answers the call.

If the interviewer has asked you to call them:

➤ Ensure you have the correct telephone number.

➤ Ensure you call at precisely the time they have designated.

➤ Ensure you leave a message if you are unable to get through.

Video-conferencing and webcam-based interviews

More and more employers are looking to harness tools such as video-conferencing and the Internet to facilitate the interviewing process.

If meeting in person is impractical (or, for whatever reason, undesirable) then, provided both you and your interviewer have access to appropriate technology, you might find yourself expected to participate in such an interview.

First and foremost you need to ensure you fully understand how to use the technology in question. It will not create a good impression if you agree to an interview of this nature and then struggle to deal with the technology.

Apart from this, such interviews are very little different from 'traditional' interviews. You will be in full view of the interviewer (or interviewers) so dress appropriately, maintain a reasonable level of eye contact, smile, articulate clearly, and behave precisely as you would in any other interview.

Because you will be responsible for controlling your own environment, make sure that nobody disturbs you during the interview. If somebody walks in on you during the interview, then it is going to reflect very badly on you. This also means switching mobile phones to silent mode and taking other phones off the hook.

PART 3

ASSESSMENT CENTRES

Chapter **17**

Assessment centres

Most job hunters will never have heard of an assessment centre. It conjures up an image of a concrete bunker in the middle of a forest where you spend your days tackling assault courses and having your face shoved in the mud – at least that's the image that sprang to my mind when I was first invited to attend an assessment centre!

As it happens, this image couldn't be further from the truth. For a start, an assessment centre generally isn't a 'centre' at all. It's a term used to describe an event that will commonly take place at an organisation's premises, and is unlikely to last more than one day but can sometimes last up to three days. It doesn't involve assault courses either; it's normally just a mishmash of other, better-known interview scenarios. So even if you have not been invited to an assessment centre (yet!), you may still find some of the information in this chapter useful for other situations.

Assessment centres are increasingly popular with employers from many large corporations, either in the initial or final stages of the recruitment process, and are particularly used to assist in graduate recruitment drives. They are also used in the public sector; for example, the police force. So you need to know what to expect.

Hosting an assessment centre is certainly a major undertaking on an employer's part; it is costly both from a financial perspective and in terms of the amount of people involved in planning and running the event. But it's a very effective technique for employers to thoroughly assess a large number of candidates in a variety of situations in a short space of time. It enables them to determine, with some confidence, which candidates it will be worth investing in further by ensuring that they meet the job competencies.

What to expect at an assessment centre

All of the interview scenarios I've described so far could come into play at an assessment centre.

You could have a one-on-one interview. You could have a panel interview. You will certainly undergo group interviews.

You may be faced with aptitude tests, psychometric tests, case studies, group exercises, and be expected to give a presentation.

You have to be prepared for all of this – and more.

Facing a number of different challenges over a prolonged period of time can be extremely daunting. However, if you feel a particular activity did not go well for you, there is the opportunity to still make a good impression by succeeding in one of the other exercises.

How to prepare for an assessment centre

The best advice I can give is be prepared for all the scenarios I have covered in the previous chapters. I have also included some top tips for the types of activity that are commonly included in an assessment centre.

> **TOP TIP**
> ....
>
> If this all sounds a little extreme then keep it to yourself. Employers can take these sorts of exercise very seriously indeed!

Group interviews/group exercises

Group interviews or group exercises will probably occupy a large proportion of your time at an assessment centre.

A group exercise enables employers to assess the skills that you would be required to demonstrate in the workplace, such as communication, teamwork, leadership and problem solving. Crucial to success in this particular activity are the following:

➤ Confidence – make sure that you contribute and add value to the team but without being seen to dominate.

➤ Be sure that you listen to and respect the viewpoints of other members of the group, even if you do not necessarily agree with them. Be prepared to compromise your position for the good of the group.

➤ Make your voice heard but not to the extent that it drowns out all others.

➤ Above all, make sure the group remains focused on the overall aim of the exercise.

Preparing for a group exercise is something that you can do every day either in your current workplace or in your place of study. Practice being diplomatic in difficult situations you encounter. Take the time to listen to your colleagues/peers and ensure that if you have something to contribute, you do so with confidence. After all, these are attributes that will serve you well in any situation, not just an assessment centre.

In-tray or e-tray tests

There are many other tests an employer may use to gauge your capabilities, one of the more popular being what is known as 'in-tray' or, increasingly, 'e-tray'.

The concept is very straightforward. You will be presented with a 'typical' in-tray (or email inbox) containing various items that require your attention. These could include telephone messages, letters, reports, documents and emails. The goal is to read through all of this information as quickly as you can and to ensure that you prioritise your in-tray effectively. You will be expected to explain what the most appropriate action is to deal with each item – whether that involves actioning it yourself, delegating it or postponing it. And you'll normally be up against the clock – typical in-tray tests last between 30 minutes and an hour. It's just like real life!

You can prepare for this kind of test quite easily by ensuring that you brush up on the latest techniques for time management. There are even online resources available that enable you to practice in-tray exercises. (Please visit **www.jamesinn.es** for access to online resources which supplement this book.) Above all, the in-tray items that you will be faced with will invariably be related to the type of role you are applying for. So doing your research on the company and the role is really important.

Case studies

Another favourite is the 'case study'. You will be presented with details of a realistic situation you are likely to encounter at work, and expected to report back your thoughts, findings and recommendations, either by way of a written report or in a verbal presentation. This is your opportunity to really show the employer how well you can perform the role – rather than an interview where you are just telling them what you can do.

For the case study exercise, you may be required to work on your own or in small groups. A specific scenario will be presented to you, which you will need to carefully analyse before presenting your proposed solution.

Crucial to a successful case study is an accurate understanding of the scenario you are asked to investigate. You may well deliver a killer presentation at the end of it, but if you have missed the point of the exercise you are unlikely to be successful.

Preparation may be difficult because you do not know what situation you will be presented with. After all, the aim of a case study is for an employer to see how you cope with the unfamiliar. As with the other activities, researching the company and the position you are applying for is always helpful. And on the day, make sure you take the time to read all of the information that you are given.

Top tips for delivering winning presentations

Assessment centres will invariably require you to deliver a presentation of some form, whether individually or as part of a case study or group exercise. Whilst presentations can be nerve-wracking, you can certainly maximise your chances of success on the day with the following tips:

➤ Structure your presentation carefully with a clearly defined beginning, middle and end so that you don't lose your way.

➤ Always keep the timeframe in mind when preparing the presentation. Make sure the content is not too long (or too short).

➤ Deliberately slow your speech down. Nerves can make you talk quicker than you normally would and you want to make sure that you get your point across clearly and articulately.

➤ Use visual aids where appropriate to emphasise your key points but don't make them too wordy.

➤ Smile, and engage with your audience by varying the tone of your voice.

Please refer back to Chapter 14: Presentations for further advice on this topic.

Assessment centres can be demanding but they can also be great fun! Do your best to enjoy this unique opportunity to showcase your skills and you will be sure to come across well.

PART 4

INTERVIEW QUESTIONS – AND THEIR ANSWERS!

Chapter **18**

Basic principles

Obviously, no one can know exactly what questions will be asked at interview but there are certain topics that will almost certainly come up.

However, before we start looking at some of the questions you might be asked, I'd like to cover some important ground rules.

Listen!

It's actually surprisingly easy for your thoughts to stray elsewhere and for you to fail to listen properly to a question. You're in a stressful situation and you have a lot on your mind; it's perfectly possible to get distracted. If you do fail to hear a question properly, then don't be afraid to ask the interviewer to repeat the question. It's not ideal but it's certainly better than failing to fully answer the question – or guessing at what you've been asked, going off at a tangent and giving the answer to a totally different question!

It's also possible that you might fail to understand a question the first time around. Again, don't be afraid to ask the interviewer to repeat or to clarify the question. At the very least it gives you valuable extra thinking time. But don't make a habit of it.

Try to understand the meaning behind the question

Why have they asked you this question? What is it they are trying to find out?

I wouldn't go so far as to say that all interview questions have hidden meanings, but it is true that the intentions of the interviewer might not immediately be apparent from the question. If you can work out the meaning behind the question, then you are at least 80 per cent of the way towards determining the optimum answer.

There are three key areas that interviewers will be considering when matching a vacancy with the best possible candidate.

➤ Can you do the job? Do you have what it takes?

➤ Will you do the job? Or will you just go through the motions?

➤ Do you fit in with the other employees and the organisation as a whole?

All of their questions will address one of these three areas in one way or another. Therefore, in trying to understand the meaning behind any particular question you need to first identify which of the above areas the interviewer is trying to tackle.

Beyond that, you need to make sure you see the world from the interviewer's point of view. When asking you a particular question, what exactly is going through their mind?

Different types of question

As well as questions probing different areas, there are also different ways in which interviewers phrase their questions. You need to be aware of the different techniques they will use because it will naturally impact on the way you answer.

In general terms, most questions can be classified as either 'open' or 'closed'.

A 'closed' question is one which can be answered very quickly – often with just one word.

> ➤ Are you creative?
> ➤ Do you thrive under pressure?
> ➤ Are you a risk taker?
> ➤ Do you have sales experience?

An 'open' question, on the other hand, is one that will force a lengthier answer.

> ➤ In what ways would you say that you are creative?
> ➤ Can you tell me about a time when you were under significant pressure and how you handled it?
> ➤ How do you feel about taking risks?
> ➤ Can you tell me about your sales experience?

A good interviewer will normally ask mainly open questions because these are the questions that will extract the most useful information from you. Conversely, a poor interviewer is likely to ask you a much higher proportion of closed questions.

Regardless of the type of question (or interviewer) you're faced with, you should always avoid 'yes' and 'no' answers to questions unless you're sure it's appropriate – because they tend to be conversation stoppers.

TOP TIP

· ·

A single-word answer doesn't give you any scope to sell yourself; consequently, it's of no benefit either to yourself or to the interviewer. If an interviewer does ask you a closed question, don't let their inexperience as an interviewer jeopardise your chances of getting your message across. Rework the question in your own mind so that you are actually answering an open form of the question.

Leading questions

Another type of question you are likely to encounter is the 'leading' question.

➤ What character flaws do you have?

➤ Why haven't you achieved more in your career?

➤ You must surely have more than one weakness?

You can see that these questions, whilst open, nevertheless lead you down a very specific path. The interviewer isn't asking you whether or not you have any character flaws; in delivering a leading question they are making it clear they have inherently assumed that you do indeed have character flaws. Leading questions are definitely something you need to keep a close lookout for.

You should also note that a leading question doesn't always have to be an open question. By posing you a leading question which is also a closed question an interviewer can really put you on the spot:

➤ I think you're overqualified for this job. Don't you?

Funnel interviewing

A final interviewing technique I'd like to make you aware of is so-called 'funnel' interviewing.

In funnel interviewing, an interviewer will first pose you a very general question about a topic (potentially lulling you into a false sense of security) before following up their original question with more and more precise questions (often based on your previous answers) on the same topic until you are talking about precisely what interests them.

It's a popular interrogation technique, but it's not as frightening as it sounds. It all depends on the interviewer. Generally their supplementary questions will follow a fairly mundane sequence, starting with the favourite, 'Can you give me an example?'

The secret to handling this technique is simply to be aware of it and to make sure that you don't let the interviewer force you into revealing anything that's not to your advantage.

Engage brain before opening mouth! (EBBOM)

Think before you speak!

Pause to give yourself the necessary time to construct an answer, so that you answer the question to the best of your ability. If you've prepared properly – and both this and the following chapters should help you to do just that – then it's unlikely any question will come as too much of a shock to you. You should already have an answer more or less ready.

However, if you're taken aback by the question then do give yourself a few seconds before starting to respond. That should be just long enough to get your head around the question and will make a big difference to the quality of your answer.

Keep your answer on track

Make sure that you answer questions fully without waffling or chattering on unnecessarily. Nervousness can all too easily cause you to say too much and to give too much away.

Besides your own nervousness, another reason you are likely to say more than you should is an interviewing technique whereby the interviewer waits for you to finish your answer and then doesn't immediately follow up with another question. They just sit there silently. It's human nature for you to then carry on talking, either elaborating on your existing answer or rephrasing your answer just to fill the awkward silence.

This is a technique popular with sales negotiators, because forcing someone to say more than they originally intended to say will generally weaken their position. It's also a technique used by psychotherapists.

They are trained to say very little because this forces you to say more – and hence to open up and disclose more. Whilst this might be very useful for someone undergoing psychotherapy, it's likely to cause you to come unstuck in an interview. Be aware of this technique and don't fall into the trap.

An interviewer is especially likely to adopt this tactic after a question such as, 'What are your weaknesses?' The more they can keep you talking, the more you're likely to reveal.

Back up your answers with real-life examples

Wherever possible you should try to integrate real-life examples into your answers rather than just speaking hypothetically. Flagging up specific relevant examples from your own experience is an ideal way of reinforcing your points in the interviewer's mind.

TOP TIP

If the interviewer asks you a straightforward question without specifically requesting you to give an example, then don't hesitate to be proactive and give an example anyway.

I've already made the point that many interviewers will start with a simple question then probe the topic further by following up with another question, such as, 'Can you give me an example?'

If you pre-empt this by illustrating your initial response with an example then it's bound to impress them.

Delivering sound bites

If you watch a politician or a senior businessman being interviewed on television then you will notice that they all have a little trick up their sleeve. If they've received any kind of debate or media training they will be adept at making sure they get their point across regardless of the question being asked. This is especially so when they're discussing particularly sensitive topics or when confronted with a particularly aggressive interviewer.

In his famous interview with politician Michael Howard, interviewer Jeremy Paxman asked exactly the same question – 'Did you threaten to overrule him?' – 12 times without getting a straight answer!

It's vital that you should not be seen as being this evasive. It didn't do much for Michael Howard's reputation and it won't do much for yours! However, if you are able to subtly steer a question around so as to dodge an issue you are uncomfortable with – and deliver a pre-prepared statement you have been keen to make – then it can be a very effective technique. But use it sparingly.

You may not be answering the precise question you have been asked but you should be addressing the topic that the interviewer has raised. You're simply doing so in the manner that suits you best.

The truth, the whole truth…

Never lie at interview or say something that you cannot substantiate.

For many candidates their troubles start even before they've been invited for the interview because a large percentage of people seem to think it's permissible to tell a few small porkies when writing their CV. Many think it's acceptable because 'everyone else does it', and it is a fact that many prospective employers do not check an applicant's information as thoroughly as they perhaps should.

I would always strongly caution anyone against telling anything but the truth on their CV. You can easily become unstuck during an interview as a result.

BLOOPER!

One candidate wrongly claimed to be fluent in French on his CV and got quite a shock when he came up against a half-French, half-English interviewer who thought it quite reasonable to conduct the interview in French!

It's not going to do you much good to be worrying about whether or not you are going to be unmasked as a liar. This is a surprisingly common cause of pre-interview jitters.

STATISTIC

....

Surveys show that approximately 30 per cent of candidates 'lie' to one degree or another at interview.

It all depends, of course, on how you define 'lie'. Twenty per cent engage in a 'significant' lie – the kind where you could later be sacked for gross misconduct as a result, whereas up to 35 per cent include at least one small porky here or there.

Just because 'everyone else does it' it doesn't mean you should. Not everyone lies – it remains a minority – and it is questionable whether those that do gain any benefit from it.

Whether or not you tell the 'whole' truth, though, is another matter entirely. Clearly you should always put as positive a spin on matters, but it's a fine line and only you can really be the judge of what is and is not acceptable.

Don't be a parrot

An essential warning to all readers

I will be giving you example answers to a whole variety of questions, but I must emphasise that it is vitally important for you to think through and write out your own answers. Once I have fully explained to you the meaning behind the question and given you my pointers on how to develop your own answer, it shouldn't be too difficult for you to do so.

My examples are purely there to help illustrate the points made; they're there to act as a guide only and most are unlikely to be relevant to your precise circumstances. It's essential for you to think for yourself and create your own answers; my job is to help you achieve that.

This will, of course, take some time and effort on your part, but it is absolutely vital as your answers must come across as genuine. It's time and effort that will really pay dividends. You'll feel so much more confident.

Too many candidates make the mistake of sounding as if they're reciting from some old-fashioned book on interview technique, such as *101 Interview Questions*.

Make sure you don't fall into this trap. This is really important. There are no universally 'right' answers to interview questions – just answers that are right for *you* – and I will help *you* to work out what those right answers should be.

Even if you have prepared and memorised your own answers, you should be careful to make sure that your delivery is natural, not stilted, and doesn't come across as rehearsed. This is especially important with the more difficult and challenging questions. If you don't express any surprise and answer perfectly without hesitation, then it's going to look rather suspicious!

Chapter **19**

The ten questions you're most likely to be asked

Here's a list of what I consider to be the top ten questions you are likely to be asked at interview. Make sure you think through your answers to all these questions very carefully before going anywhere near an interview room.

1 Tell me about your work experience – what did you do, what did you enjoy, what were you good at, why did you leave each job?

2 Why have you applied for this vacancy?

3 Why do you wish to leave your current position?

4 Why do you want to work for this organisation?

5 What are your strengths?

6 What are your weaknesses?

7 What has been your greatest achievement in your personal life as well as in your career?

8 What can you, above all the other applicants, bring to this job?

9 Where do you see yourself in five years' time?

10 You've mentioned x under *Interests and activities* on your CV. Can you tell me a bit more about that?

You are absolutely certain to get asked at least some of these questions (or variations of them), if not the whole lot.

I could add an eleventh question to the list: 'And do you have any questions for me/us?' There aren't many interviews that conclude without this question being asked. But we'll come to that in Chapter 24: Your own questions.

For now, let's concentrate on the questions above.

We'll look at them one by one, alongside possible alternatives and other closely related questions. We'll analyse the interviewer's intentions in asking you the question – the meaning behind the question – and we'll discuss how best you can answer it.

Top question: can you tell me a bit about yourself?

Alternative and related questions

➤ Can you talk me through your CV?

The meaning behind the question

This is an extremely popular question, and is just the kind an interviewer might throw at you at the beginning of an interview to get the ball rolling. They are quite simply placing you centre stage and hoping you will open up to them. Alternatively, they are hopelessly overworked, haven't yet had time to read your CV, and asking you this question will buy them some breathing space!

Your answer

This is a very broad question, and you might, therefore, be at a loss as to the approach you should take to answering it.

They are not asking for an autobiography. Focus on discussing major selling points that feature on your CV or application form; selling points that are directly relevant to the job for which you are applying. Don't start telling your whole life history.

Whilst they do want you to open up and paint a picture of yourself, you're not on the psychiatrist's couch here! Keep it professional and avoid getting too personal.

Besides talking about your career, make sure that you have something to say about your education and qualifications and even your hobbies and interests.

EXAMPLE

I'm a highly driven individual with extensive management experience acquired principally in the aviation sector. Following completion of my degree in International Business (which included a couple of years in Germany), I started my career in administration and have worked my way up to become an export sales manager. I believe I combine a high level of commercial awareness with a commitment to customer care, which helps me to achieve profitable growth in a competitive market. I enjoy being part of, as well as managing, motivating, training and developing, a successful and productive team and I thrive in highly pressurised and challenging working environments. I have strong IT skills, I'm fluent in German and I'm also a qualified first aider. In my spare time I undertake a wide range of activities; I'm particularly keen on squash and I am also currently working towards my Private Pilot Licence.

It's vital to practise your answer for this in advance, and try to limit your answer to one minute. If you can't successfully 'pitch' yourself in under a minute you risk losing the interviewer's attention.

How have you described yourself in the professional profile at the top of your CV? A lot of this material can be recycled to help you draft your answer to this question.

2 Why have you applied for this vacancy?

Alternative and related questions

➤ Why do you want this vacancy?

➤ What attracted you to this vacancy?

➤ Why do you think you're suitable for this job?

➤ What is it that you are looking for in a new job?

The meaning behind the question

The interviewer is probing to see

➤ If you fully understand what the job entails

➤ How well you might match their requirements

➤ What appeals to you most about the job

Your answer

This is another open-ended question where you might be tempted to say too much. By taking the time to think through your answer to this question in advance, you will be able to remain focused on a few key points.

Your emphasis should be on demonstrating to the interviewer precisely how you match their requirements and, in doing so, demonstrate that you fully understand what the role entails.

If you've done your research properly (please see Chapter 2: Researching the job), then you will have a good idea of what it is the company is looking for.

You have been asked what your motivations are in applying for the vacancy, but try to turn the question round so that the answer you give indicates why you are the right candidate for the vacancy.

THE TEN QUESTIONS YOU'RE MOST LIKELY TO BE ASKED

> ### EXAMPLE
>
> I've applied for this vacancy because it's an excellent match for my skills and experience and because it represents a challenge I know I'll relish. I already have extensive experience as a senior quantity surveyor, including previous experience of rail and station projects – an area I'm particularly interested in. I enjoy managing multiple projects simultaneously. I also enjoy overseeing and coaching junior and assistant quantity surveyors. I'm used to dealing directly with clients; developing productive working relationships with clients is definitely one of my strengths. This is exactly the type of role I am currently targeting and I am confident I will be able to make a major contribution.

3 Why do you wish to leave your current position?

Alternative and related questions

➤ Why do you wish to leave your current employer?

➤ What do you plan to say to your current employer in your letter of resignation?

The meaning behind the question

The interviewer is trying to understand your motivation for changing jobs. They clearly want to know why you want to change jobs but they also want to know how serious you are about changing jobs. Are you really committed to moving or are you just wasting their time?

Your answer

There are a multitude of reasons for wanting to leave your job; however, they won't all be positive selling points for you.

Positive reasons include:

➤ Wanting a greater challenge

➤ Wanting to diversify

➤ Seeking greater opportunities

➤ Seeking further advancement

➤ Taking a step up the career ladder.

Negative reasons include:

➤ Problems with your boss

➤ Problems with a colleague

➤ A financially unstable organisation

➤ Personal reasons.

If your reason for wanting to leave your job is a positive one, then your answer will be easy enough to construct. Explain to the interviewer what your motivations are and how the move to your next job will help you to achieve your goals. You are making a positive move for positive reasons and intend to achieve a positive outcome simple as that.

If, however, your reason for leaving your job is in my list of negative reasons, then giving the right answer is going to be somewhat trickier. Because each situation is so different, I will deal with each of them in turn.

Problems with your boss: Having problems with the boss is the top reason people give (in surveys) for changing jobs. However, you should never say anything negative about either a current or a previous employer. It isn't professional, it doesn't portray you as someone who is particularly loyal, and it will reflect badly on you. In almost all cases, I would recommend that you avoid citing this as a reason. Criticising your current employer is considered one of the top mistakes you can make at interview and will most likely cost you the job regardless of whether or not your criticism is justified. Aim to give an answer that focuses on the benefits you will experience in moving to your new job rather than making any reference to your having had problems with your boss.

BLOOPER!

Having delivered a particularly devastating critique of his current employer, one candidate was rather shocked to discover that his current employer was in fact the interviewer's brother-in-law!

Problems with a colleague: Maybe you want to leave because of a persistently unpleasant colleague? However, explaining this to the interviewer will most likely open you up to expressing bitterness or recrimination – traits that are not attractive to a potential employer. Again, you should aim to give an answer that focuses on the benefits of moving to your new job rather than drawing attention to your problems.

A financially unstable organisation: You may well have decided to leave your job before your employer finally goes bankrupt, but you don't want to be labelled as a rat leaving a sinking ship. It doesn't say much for your loyalty. Avoid giving this as a reason.

Personal reasons: There are many different personal circumstances that might cause you to wish to leave a job. For example, you might simply want a better work–life balance. However, if possible you should avoid giving 'personal reasons' as an answer and instead leave the interviewer to believe you are leaving in order to pursue a more promising opportunity.

As for asking what you would write in a resignation letter, you should remember that when it comes to resignation letters it is well worth being as nice as possible about the matter. Harsh words in a letter of resignation could easily come back to haunt you in the future – not least if you ever need a reference from this employer.

EXAMPLE

After careful consideration, I have made the decision to move on to a new challenge. Naturally, I'd thank them for the opportunities with which they presented me during the course of my employment, reassure them that I will do my best to help ensure the seamless transfer of my duties and responsibilities before leaving and wish them all the very best for the future.

4 Why do you want to work for this organisation?

Alternative and related questions

➤ What is it about our organisation that attracts you?

The meaning behind the question

The interviewer is analysing your motivations and probing your expectations of the organisation. Why do you want to work for this one in particular? Whilst this question doesn't directly ask what you know about their organisation, in order to be able to answer it effectively you are clearly going to have to demonstrate that you have done your homework.

Your answer

If you have done your research properly (please see Chapter 3: Researching the organisation), you will already be fairly well informed as to the organisation you are applying to join. However, the key to answering this question is how to communicate that knowledge to the interviewer whilst tying it in with why you want to work for them.

Focus on what in particular attracts you to the organisation. We'll cover the closely related but more generalised question, 'What do you know about us as an organisation?' in the next chapter.

> **EXAMPLE**
>
> I'm particularly attracted by how progressive an organisation you are. I've seen how your sales levels have grown the past few years and I'm aware of your plans to expand into the United States. Yours is an organisation that is rapidly developing and evolving, that's exactly what I'm looking for. I want to work for an organisation which is forward-thinking and isn't afraid to tackle new challenges.

5 What are your strengths?

Alternative and related questions

➤ What are you good at?

➤ What do you consider yourself to be good at?

The meaning behind the question

With this question the interviewer wants to achieve the following:

➤ Identify what your key selling points are.

➤ Establish whether or not these strengths are relevant to the role they are interviewing for.

➤ Gain some insight into your character – how self-confident (or arrogant) you are.

Your answer

Everyone has their strengths. The key to answering this question is not to rattle off a long list of what you consider your strengths to be. Instead, you should be looking to highlight a smaller number of specific strengths, discussing each one briefly and, most importantly, identifying how these strengths relate to the requirements of the job you are applying to undertake. You can even elaborate on one of your strengths by mentioning a specific relevant achievement.

Choose your strengths carefully. It can be hard to say anything very interesting, for example, about the fact that you are very meticulous and pay great attention to detail. However, if the recruiter is looking for someone to lead a team, then you can mention team leadership as one of your strengths, citing an appropriate example or achievement.

Word of warning

If you don't give the interviewer at least one specific example to back up your statement, be prepared for them to ask for one!

EXAMPLE

I believe my key strength is that I combine experience of traditional film production with extensive experience in the online arena. I'm very aware of current trends in new media and am able to demonstrate excellent creative judgement. I'm also very good at juggling multiple projects simultaneously; in my current role I frequently have as many as half a dozen different projects on the go at any one time, and I'm committed to completing them all on time and on budget. This clearly requires extremely strong project management skills.

6 What are your weaknesses?

Alternative and related questions

➤ What are you not good at doing?

➤ What do you find difficult to do and why?

➤ In what areas do you feel you need to improve?

The meaning behind the question

With questions of this kind the interviewer wants to achieve the following:

➤ Identify any weakness which might actually be detrimental to your ability to undertake the role.

➤ See how you react when faced with a somewhat tricky question.

➤ Assess how self-aware you are and how you define weakness.

Your answer

Yes, this is a tricky one. Whilst it is superficially a somewhat negative question, it is in fact full of opportunities for you to turn it around to your advantage and make your answer a positive point.

Don't be perturbed by the question or let it throw you off balance. Your answer should be right on the tip of your tongue. You should only ever discuss a professional weakness, unless the interviewer specifically requests otherwise (unlikely).

Your first thought might be to say, 'I don't really have any particular weaknesses.' But this is definitely not the answer the interviewer is looking for – and is definitely not the answer you should be giving.

BLOOPER!

Telling the interviewer your weakness is 'kryptonite' – as one candidate did – is unlikely to amuse an interviewer. But it may possibly be better than the candidate who said he was a 'work*alco*holic'!

The interviewer wants to know that you are able to look at yourself objectively and to criticise yourself where appropriate. If you honestly don't think you have any weaknesses and say so, then you risk coming across as arrogant, and nobody wants a perfect candidate anyway.

Clearly, you don't just want to come up with a straightforward list of what you consider your weaknesses to be, so you have two choices:

➤ Talk about a weakness that's not necessarily a weakness at all.

➤ Talk about a weakness that you turned (or can turn) into a strength.

The problem with the first option is that you risk running into cliché territory. I'm talking about the kind of people who answer:

➤ I would have to say that my main weakness is that I'm a perfectionist.

➤ I have a reputation for working too hard; I often push myself far too hard in my work.

You risk sounding as though you plucked your answer straight out of a 1990s manual on interview technique.

Personally, I prefer the second option: talking about a weakness that you turned (or are turning) into a strength because you are answering the interviewer's question by highlighting a definite weakness, before reflecting positively on it by outlining the active steps you are taking to overcome it. You are demonstrating a willingness to learn, adapt and improve, and you are showing that you have the initiative required to make changes where changes are due.

Choosing a weakness that has its root in lack of experience and has been (or is being) overcome by further training is ideal because it is a weakness that is relatively easily resolved.

EXAMPLE

When I started my current job my first few months were an uphill battle dealing with a backlog of work I inherited from my predecessor. I recognised that I have a weakness when it comes to time management. I have since been on a time management course, read a couple of books on the subject and I believe I've made a lot of progress. But it's something I'm still very vigilant about. I make a concerted effort to apply the principles I've learned every day and to put in place procedures which enable me to most effectively prioritise and process my workload.

This example is a good and comprehensive answer meeting all the objectives we've outlined above.

Word of warning

Do be prepared for the interviewer to ask the follow-up question, 'OK. That's one weakness. You must have more than one weakness?'

---

7 What has been your greatest achievement/accomplishment?

Alternative and related questions

➤ What are your biggest achievements?

➤ What are you most proud of?

➤ What was your biggest achievement in your current/last job?

➤ What has been the high point of your career so far?

The meaning behind the question

Unless the question is qualified by specifically mentioning, for example, your last job, it is important to remember that the interviewer isn't necessarily looking for a work-related achievement. They are looking for evidence of achievement, full stop. However, a work-related achievement is normally what they will be expecting.

Your answer

Make sure you have thought this question through carefully before the interview and have selected both a key professional achievement as well as a key personal achievement to cover both bases.

Try not to go too far back; try to pick a recent achievement. If you've included an achievements section in your CV (which I would recommend you do) then this will be a good starting point for you to generate ideas.

Describe clearly to the interviewer

➤ What it is that you achieved

➤ What the background and circumstances were

➤ What impact it had on your career/life

What was the benefit? Try to phrase this in such a way for it to be self-evident that this would also be a benefit to any prospective employer.

My greatest achievement so far in my career would probably be winning the manager of the year award last year. I made numerous operational changes at my branch, including a massive reduction in stock levels, which significantly boosted our working capital. I also drove up sales levels, especially by increasing the uptake of after-sales insurance packages. The net effect was that we smashed the previous branch sales record by an impressive 37 per cent and profits rose in line with this. This directly resulted in my promotion to the management of the flagship Edinburgh branch.

8 What can you, above all the other applicants, bring to this job?

Alternative and related questions

➤ What makes you the best candidate for this job?

The meaning behind the question

The interviewer is directly asking what your 'unique selling point' is. They are looking for at least one significant reason that you should be their No. 1 choice for the job.

Your answer

Well, what does make you the best candidate for this job?

I'll level with you – this isn't necessarily a top ten question in terms of how likely you are to get asked it. However, it is very much a top ten question in terms of the importance of your having prepared an answer to it. You need to go into every interview with a thorough understanding of what it is that you have to offer. If you don't know what it is that you're offering then how can you hope to sell it effectively?

If you do get asked this specific question, then don't be afraid to answer it quite candidly. It's a bold question and warrants a bold answer. The interviewer is putting you on the spot to sell yourself. But do be very careful to avoid coming across as arrogant because that's the last thing you want to do. It's a fine line you need to tread.

Feel free to cite an example from your past where you demonstrated that you are someone who is capable of going the extra mile. It's all very well to say that you're someone who gives 110 per cent (although it is a bit of a cliché), but if you can actually throw an example at your interviewer then you're going to be a whole lot more credible.

BLOOPER!

An ex-army candidate for a management role replied, 'I can shoot someone at 300 yards.' What is more amazing is that he actually got the job! This is a rare example of a sense of humour working to the candidate's advantage.

EXAMPLE

Having now been working in this industry for over a decade, I have developed successful relationships with key decision makers in numerous companies, enabling me to achieve a sales conversion rate much higher than average. This is undoubtedly a very challenging role, requiring considerable drive and determination, but I believe my previous sales record is clear evidence that I am more than capable of achieving what it is that you need.

---

9 Where do you see yourself in five years' time?

Alternative and related questions

➤ How long do you plan to stay/would you stay in this job if we offer it to you?

➤ What are your long-term career goals?

➤ How does this job fit into your long-term career plans?

➤ How far do you feel you might progress in our organisation?

The meaning behind the question

The interviewer is trying to ascertain what your long-term career ambitions are and to get a better understanding of your motivations. They will invariably be looking for someone who is keen to learn, develop and progress. However, they are recruiting for a specific role and will want someone who is prepared to commit to that role for a reasonable period of time.

You may think this question is just a cliché and doesn't really get asked in practice. Trust me it does and far more frequently than you might imagine.

Your answer

Lots of people think they're displaying a great sense of humour/ambition/self-confidence to reply, 'Doing your job!' I wouldn't recommend it because it may come across as arrogant and aggressive.

Avoid being too specific. It's very difficult for most people to know exactly what job they will be undertaking in five years and so it can be unrealistic to quote a specific job title you are aiming for. Try to present your answer more in terms of what level you hope to have reached – what level of responsibility, of autonomy. It's also a good idea if you can phrase your answer to communicate that you hope still to be with this same organisation in five years' time.

EXAMPLE

Five years from now I expect I will have progressed significantly in my career and be making an even greater contribution. Having proved my value to the organisation I would hope to have been given increased responsibilities and greater challenges. I've clearly given a good deal of thought to working for you and I can see that there are indeed a lot of opportunities both for promotion and for ongoing professional development. My career is very important to me and I want to push myself hard to deliver the very best of which I'm capable.

10 You've mentioned x under *Interests and activities* on your CV. Can you tell me a bit more about that?

Alternative and related questions

> What activities do you enjoy outside work?

> What are you interested in outside work?

The meaning behind the question

There are a variety of possible reasons interviewers might ask this question.

> They're trying to get some insight into your personality and character.

> They're testing to see how truthful you've been on your CV.

> They've run out of other questions and are killing time!

Besides knowing whether you're capable of doing the job, most employers are keen to know what sort of a person you are to work alongside. Employers are generally keen to have a diversity of characters within their team and are always on the lookout for someone who can add a new dimension.

Whilst nobody has yet conducted a survey specifically to research this, there is plenty of anecdotal evidence of recruiters deciding to call someone in for an interview purely as a result of what they have included in their CV under interests and activities. I, for one, will admit to having done so when hiring.

Your answer

This is a very simple question to answer provided, as always, that you've prepared for it in advance. If you have a hobby that makes for an interesting talking point at the interview then it will reflect positively on you as an individual.

Remember, you need to be able to back up everything you've listed on your CV. If you mention playing chess to give your CV some intellectual clout, but haven't played since you were at school, then you could well come a cropper in your interview if your interviewer turns out to be a chess fan and asks you which openings to the game you favour!

It's always a good idea if you can subtly slip in mention of any positions of responsibility you hold outside work. If your passion is, for example, football, and you're also the captain of the local team, then do say so.

Besides the obvious selling point of football being a team activity (and hence your being a team player), you've immediately communicated your leadership qualities, your ability to take responsibility for others, your ability to commit yourself to a project etc.

EXAMPLE

I've always been fascinated by planes. I remember my first flight as a child; it was a thrilling experience. Even though I understand the science behind it, I'm still in awe each and every time I see a plane clear the runway. It's quite an expensive hobby to pursue but, as soon as I could afford to do so, I started taking flying lessons. I gained my Private Pilot Licence, went on to qualify as an instructor and I'm now a senior member of my local flying club. Whilst it's not something I've ever wished to pursue as a career, I do enjoy giving the occasional lesson and generally participating in the club community. It's definitely something about which I'm very passionate.

Chapter **20**

Forty classic questions you must be prepared for

There are a number of interview question books which feature hundreds of different questions and answers. Whilst you might have time to quickly read through them, you're unlikely to have the time or the inclination to look at any of them in any great depth, nor to think through your own answers to the questions.

If you look closely at all those questions, you'll see that many of them are simply variations on a theme and that the same core themes come up again and again. There are many different ways to word a question but only a limited number of topics the interviewer is likely to be interested in.

I believe that rather than spoon-feeding you the answers to hundreds of questions, it's much more important for you to recognise and fully understand the different lines of questioning an interviewer is likely to take.

Within each theme there will be a cluster of closely related questions all designed to address the same issue.

I have condensed hundreds of interview questions down to a list of 40 questions, which cover pretty much every key issue an interviewer is likely to tackle you on. We'll be looking at these in detail in this chapter.

So-called 'tough' questions

Questions which you might, at first sight, consider to be tough are actually nothing more than alternatively and more aggressively phrased versions of classic questions.

For example, instead of asking you the relatively innocuous question, 'How far do you feel you might rise in our organisation?' your interviewer, if they are the sadistic sort, might ask you, 'Would you like to have my job?'

Clearly, there will be differences in how you respond to each of these questions but the core answer is the same.

I'm not saying that tough questions don't exist; they most certainly do. However, most of the questions you're likely to encounter, which might traditionally be seen as tough, really aren't once you've understood what the interviewer is driving at. If you can see through to the meaning behind the question, then it can take a lot of the sting out of it.

1 How would you describe yourself?/How would your boss/colleagues/team/family/friends describe you?

Alternative and related questions

➤ What do you think your references will say about you?

➤ What kind of person are you to work with?

The meaning behind the question

The interviewer wants to assess how you perceive yourself. Whether they ask how you would describe yourself or how others would describe you, the question is all about your perception of yourself; seeing yourself as others see you.

Your answer

This is a very popular question and could have made my top ten. It's vital to be prepared for it.

Make sure you have a few well-chosen adjectives up your sleeve ready to answer this question, e.g. loyal, dedicated, ambitious, determined, independent, highly motivated, understanding. Tell the interviewer what they want to hear! But don't be too big-headed; a little modesty can go a long way.

It's a difficult balance to strike but I hope the following example will show you how to achieve this.

EXAMPLE

I would describe myself as a very determined and highly motivated person. I do take my job seriously but I'm able to see things in perspective and believe I'm quite easy-going to work with. I'm an optimist rather than a pessimist. I'm also a realist and I cope well when the going gets tough; I'm very good at finding solutions to problems. Above all, I would say I'm a positive and enthusiastic person, and I relish a challenge.

Word of warning

There's no need to back up this answer with examples, such as outlining a time when you were particularly understanding with a colleague. It would be going too far.

---

2 In what ways are you a team player?

Alternative and related questions

➤ Do you prefer working on your own or as part of a team?

➤ How would you define teamwork?

➤ Can you tell me about a team you worked in and the role you played within that team?

➤ What do you think makes a perfect team?

The meaning behind the question

Teamwork is essential in almost any work environment. Questioning your ability to work in a team is, therefore, one of an interviewer's favourites. They will be looking for evidence of a number of core abilities.

➤ The ability to communicate effectively with others.

➤ The ability to recognise and understand the viewpoints of others.

➤ The ability to appreciate the contribution you are expected to make.

Your answer

As well as pre-preparing your answer to 'In what ways are you a team player?' you should also draft answers to all the alternative questions I've listed above. There will be common ground between your answers but each will have a slightly different slant to it.

You could answer the question in the context of your current job but you're better off approaching it from the angle of the job for which you are applying. You're being asked in what ways you are a team player, but you need to be asking yourself in what ways will they want you to be a team player? Are they looking for a leader? Are they looking for someone who brings out the best in others? Are they looking for the person who generates the ideas or the person who is a dab hand at putting new ideas into practice?

Establish in your own mind what sort of a team player they want you to be and then deliver an answer which caters to that image.

Remember, you should always be striving to become a better team player tomorrow than you are today. Here are my top ten key tips to help you become just that.

- ➤ Actively participate. Fully engage in the work of the team. Resist the temptation of sitting passively on the sidelines. Volunteer to contribute. Pitch in!

- ➤ Remember The Golden Rule: treat others as you would like others to treat you – even if you might sometimes feel they deserve otherwise!

- ➤ Treat other members of your team as individuals. Recognise and appreciate the uniqueness of their experience, knowledge, opinions and point of view.

- ➤ Don't hold back on sharing your own experience, knowledge, opinions and point of view.

- ➤ Seek to generate creativity and innovation. Promote divergent points of view. Benefit from your differences.

- ➤ Seize the initiative in finding solutions to any problems your team might encounter. People don't want problems; they want solutions.

- ➤ A problem shared is a problem halved. Let your team members know that they can come to you with problems and you'll help them to find solutions.

- ➤ Yes, it's a great cliché of business theory, but remember there is no 'I' in 'team'! What is in the best interests of the team should generally coincide with your own best interests.

- ➤ Be prepared to 'take one for the team', i.e. willingly make a personal sacrifice for the benefit of the team. There are few surer ways to get the respect of your colleagues.

- ➤ Accept the mistakes of others with good grace, and don't compound your own mistakes by trying to hide them. We all learn from our mistakes and from the mistakes of others.

I very much enjoy working with others; I'm outgoing, I enjoy the team spirit and I understand the needs of others. I'm good at helping members of the team see the bigger picture – to see the wood from the trees – helping them to focus on what really matters rather than getting bogged down in irrelevant detail. I'm also good at helping the team to spot flaws in our approach and potential problems and pitfalls. I believe I have strong communication skills and, whilst I don't yet have experience in a leadership role, I do have a talent for liaising between different team members and resolving any disputes which may arise. Conflict between different team members is rarely very productive and is normally best avoided.

3 Do you work well on your own initiative?

Alternative and related questions

➤ Are you able to manage your own workload?

The meaning behind the question

Given the choice between someone who can be left to get on with a job and someone who needs constant supervision, who would you hire?

Employees who work well on their own initiative are highly prized.

With this question, the interviewer is purely seeking evidence that you are such an employee.

Your answer

Of course you work well on your own initiative. But how can you prove that to the interviewer? This is a closed question that requires more than a one-word answer. It's a great chance for you to roll out a pre-prepared example, which ticks all the interviewer's boxes and shows you in a positive light.

If the interviewer is asking you this question, chances are you will be expected to work on your own initiative in the role you're applying for. If you've studied the job description carefully, you should be able to identify under what circumstances this will be required. Choosing an example from a past (or present) job, which closely matches these circumstances, is naturally going to have a much stronger impact.

> **EXAMPLE**
>
> I enjoy working with others but I'm equally able to work on my own initiative. I'm not afraid to ask for guidance if necessary. I'm quick to learn and, once I've understood what's required of me, I am more than capable of getting on with the job under my own steam. In my current role I work as part of a close-knit team but that's not to say that there aren't certain tasks and projects I have to handle on my own. For example, I have sole responsibility for reconciling credits and debits on our bank statements to our sales and purchase ledgers. It's not a task that can be shared with anyone; it's not a two-man job. I set aside one day a week to concentrate on this because it requires a lot of concentration, reconciling entries which match and taking steps to resolve any discrepancies.

Word of warning

Even if you do prefer to work on your own, it's best not to mention this. You don't want to risk being labelled 'not a team player'. This question doesn't ask whether you prefer to work on your own; it simply asks how capable you are of doing so.

4 What techniques do you use to get things done?

Alternative and related questions

➤ How do you get things done at work?

The meaning behind the question

This is a very simple question. The interviewer wants to know what your working style is; how do you plan and organise yourself to ensure that you achieve your objectives? They don't just want to hear that you're a very organised and efficient person, they want proof of exactly how you get things done.

Your answer

Tell it like it is. The interviewer isn't expecting any magic tricks or a treatise on the latest management techniques. Your answer just needs to outline the systems and tools you use to manage your workload to ensure that everything which needs to get done does get done. You should aim to place emphasis on this last point: the techniques you use are ones that clearly work for you.

EXAMPLE

Careful planning is critical to my ability to get things done: planning, organisation and action. I rely heavily on 'to-do' lists. These enable me to capture and record everything I need to action. I maintain a master to-do list but also have separate to-do lists for each particular project I'm handling. I review these at least once a day to identify my priorities. I always aim to focus on tasks that have deadlines attached to them and also tasks which will achieve the most in the shortest space of time. Less important items I will postpone, delegate or, if I am unable to clearly identify the benefits, remove from the list completely. Whilst I have a very heavy workload to juggle, I find that these systems enable me to always keep one step ahead and ensure that nothing slips through the net.

---

5 What motivates you?

Alternative and related questions

➤ What do you need to retain your motivation?

The meaning behind the question

What the interviewer is really asking is, 'What would we have to do to motivate you?' and 'Would you be sufficiently motivated to undertake this job effectively?' They are unlikely to ask this directly, though. By asking you the more open-ended 'What motivates you?' they are likely to extract a lot more useful information out of you – if you are careless enough to let it slip! Interviewers want to hire highly motivated people, not people who are just going to go through the motions until it's time to go home.

Your answer

There are lots of different things which could motivate you. You've got to be careful to pick factors:

➤ Which will reflect positively on you as an individual

➤ Which are not inconsistent with the job for which you are applying

➤ Which are equally of benefit to your prospective employer

➤ Which will not impose any kind of a burden on the employer

Money is, of course, a major motivator. It's the primary reason most people go to work each day! However, unless you are in sales or some other highly money-driven and largely commission-based role, then you should steer clear of mentioning money as a motivating factor. It's too selfish an answer. It's a factor that is purely in your own interests and not your prospective employer's.

I would recommend that, depending on the nature of your role, you cite factors such as challenges, results and recognition, elaborating on these to demonstrate their value to your employer.

EXAMPLE

I'm very results driven. Doing a good job and achieving the desired end result are my primary motivation. Whilst I enjoy working on a project on my own, I'm particularly motivated by the buzz of working in a team. It's very rewarding working closely with others who share the same common goal. I like to take on a challenge; I like to rise to that challenge as part of a concerted team effort, and I naturally appreciate it when my boss compliments me on a job well done.

6 Are you proactive?

Alternative and related questions

➤ How good are you at taking the initiative?

The meaning behind the question

Being proactive means making an effort to anticipate a situation and acting in advance either to prepare for it or to prevent it. It's not exactly the same as taking the initiative but the two are closely related.

In asking you this question, the interviewer wants to establish what your definition of proactive is and whether or not you are indeed proactive yourself – it is a highly desirable characteristic.

Your answer

This is a prime example of a question requiring you to deliver a specific example – whether or not the interviewer actually asks for one. If you fail to illustrate your answer with an example, then it's going to be fairly meaningless. Anyone can claim to be proactive, but can you actually prove it?

Choose your example carefully, describe the circumstances and, most importantly, explain what the benefits of your actions were.

EXAMPLE

Yes, I would consider myself to be proactive. I believe it's very important to be as proactive as possible. As the saying goes, a stitch in time saves nine! When my team is working on a project I always do my best to identify possible problems in advance and to make sure that we address them. Recently, a major project of ours was severely affected by a key member of staff leaving the company overnight (for personal reasons). I anticipated that, as a result of this, we wouldn't be able to deliver the solution to the client on time. I took the decision to contact the client, explain the situation, apologise for the delay and make the point that the quality of the finished solution was of greater importance than delivering it on schedule. The client appreciated my honesty, was very understanding and was pleased to hear that we'd never compromise on quality just to be seen to meet a deadline.

7 Are you creative?

Alternative and related questions

➤ In what ways would you say you are creative?

➤ Are you innovative/inventive?

The meaning behind the question

There's no hidden meaning here. It's a very direct question; every walk of life requires at least some degree of creativity, and creativity is often seen as an indicator of intelligence. The core question 'Are you creative?' is clearly a closed question, but answering it with a straight 'yes' isn't going to get you anywhere. Regardless of how the interviewer phrases the question, you need to say precisely in what ways you are creative, how this applies to your line of work, and to back this up with at least one example.

Your answer

Some lines of work are clearly more creative than others and the way you phrase your answer will depend on what you do for a living. If you work in a creative field, then you will need to give a much more comprehensive answer. But even if you work in a field that isn't generally seen as particularly demanding in terms of creativity, you should be able to come up with an example of where you have displayed lateral or outside-the-box thinking or invented a new and better way of handling something.

EXAMPLE

Yes, I believe I'm a creative individual. I'm certainly able to think laterally and to be inventive in terms of finding solutions to problems. Quantity surveying isn't generally seen as a particularly creative profession, but I have used my creative abilities on numerous occasions; for example, converting old manual systems of reporting to highly automated – and much more accurate – spreadsheet-based systems. This saved me and my team a considerable amount of time in the long term as well as meaning we were less exposed to the professional embarrassment of errors in our calculations.

8 Are you a risk taker?

Alternative and related questions

➤ How do you feel about taking risks?

➤ Do you have a problem with taking risks?

The meaning behind the question

'Are you a risk taker?' is a very direct question. What the interviewer is really looking for is to assess your *attitude* to taking risks. In some lines of work someone who takes risks is definitely going to be a liability, whereas in others the ability to weigh up risks – and to take *calculated* risks – is an important skill.

Your answer

Your answer will inevitably depend on exactly what the job is that you are applying for. If your line of work is one in which taking risks – or cutting corners – is likely to be frowned upon, then you're going to need to formulate your answer to make it clear that you are not someone who believes in risks. You may even want to emphasise that you see it as part of your job to identify potential risks and pre-empt them.

If assessing risks – and taking appropriate risks – is going to be a feature of your new job, then your answer will naturally be very different. You certainly want to avoid the impression of being reckless, though. Your emphasis should be on the steps you take to identify and gauge risks, only taking risks where you have calculated the potential outcomes and deemed that your actions are going to be worth the risk. You should also make some mention of your decision-making capabilities, because being prepared to take calculated risks is, ultimately, a form of decision making.

> **EXAMPLE**
>
> It depends on how you define risk. I am certainly not somebody who takes unnecessary risks, nor risks that would in any way compromise anyone's personal safety. However, I fully appreciate that commercial success is dependent on taking risks – calculated risks. If, having given a matter careful consideration and weighed up

the possible ramifications, I determine that a risk is – in the best interests of the business – worth taking, then I am not afraid to take it. You can't always be right, but careful planning and analysis should tip the odds in your favour and ensure that, overall, your decisions pay off. Experience is essential, and the experience I have gained over the course of my career is invaluable in informing my decisions.

9 How do you handle pressure and stress?

Alternative and related questions

➤ Can you tell me about a time when you were under significant pressure and how you handled that?

➤ Do you thrive under pressure?

➤ How do you cope with the numerous conflicting demands on your time?

➤ What causes you stress at work and why?

The meaning behind the question

The ability to cope with pressure and stress is essential in almost all walks of life, whether you're working on the checkout at the supermarket or heading up a major corporation. Pressure and stress are unavoidable aspects of the world we live in. The interviewer will be looking to identify:

➤ That you recognise pressure and stress are facts of life.

➤ That you understand the effect pressure and stress have on you.

➤ That you are sufficiently robust to be able to take them in your stride.

Your answer

Because of the variety of ways in which an interviewer can question you on this topic, it's important that you fully understand what the difference is between pressure and stress. Many people use the two terms interchangeably.

Being under pressure is a matter of having significant demands made of you; being challenged to achieve something that is either difficult to achieve in and of itself, or difficult to achieve within the time frame that has been set. Pressure is largely a positive force and a motivating factor for many people.

Stress, on the other hand, is not so positive. Stress occurs when the pressure you are under exceeds your ability to effectively meet the demands being made of you. Stress is what an individual experiences when exposed to excessive pressure, and long-term stress can cause all sorts of problems.

I am sure that everyone reading this book will, at some stage in their lives, have experienced pressure and stress, and know exactly what they are like.

The key to formulating your answer to this question is to seize this as an opportunity to talk about a situation or an occasion where you were under pressure, and how you rose to the challenge. Try to avoid talking about an occasion when you were totally stressed out, but do acknowledge that you understand stress and are able to deal with it appropriately.

Avoid conveying the impression that the pressure you were under was in any way your own fault, or due to your own personal failings. Place the 'blame' firmly on external factors outside your control.

Different lines of work are subject to different levels of pressure and stress and this will have a bearing on how precisely you phrase your answer.

EXAMPLE

Working for a small start-up company the past few years has naturally been quite a high-pressure experience on occasion. I've had to deal with numerous conflicting demands on my time, and often with very limited resources. With careful planning and organisation you can normally reduce the pressure you are under, but there will always be factors at play which are outside your control. Personally, whilst it makes a nice break to have a few pressure-free days, I generally thrive under pressure. I use it to help channel my energies into accomplishing as much as possible. Naturally, there are occasions when the pressure I'm put under is excessive and this can be stressful. However, I'm sufficiently experienced to appreciate that there is only so much you can reasonably be expected to be capable of, and the solution is not to panic but to remain focused on delivering your very best.

10 Can you tell me about a time when you have failed to achieve a goal?

Alternative and related questions

➤ What's the biggest failure you've experienced in your career?

➤ Can you tell me about a time when you've failed to meet an important deadline?

The meaning behind the question

As well as pinpointing a particular 'failure' in your career, the interviewer will also be gauging your overall attitude to failure – how you deal with adversity. Everyone experiences some failures during the course of their careers but not everybody bounces back and learns from the experience.

Your answer

You might think this is a tough question because there's no way to answer it without admitting failure. But it's not really that tough. The secret is to avoid picking too major a failure and, whatever example you choose, to subtly blame the failure on factors outside your control. You should be very wary indeed of laying the blame at the doorstep of a former boss or colleague; this can backfire on you spectacularly. However, you can certainly dilute some of the blame by saying that you were working 'as part of a team' at the time.

Word of warning

Don't be tempted to say you've never failed. The interviewer won't believe you!

EXAMPLE

In my last job we were given the opportunity to pitch for a major contract at relatively short notice. I was part of a team that spent a good couple of weeks working very hard on the tender and it was clear that our company was undoubtedly the best choice for the contract. Unfortunately, the client had employed a rather inexperienced individual to review the tenders and they fell for a competitor's sales pitch, which had a lot less substance but a lot more spin. It was a major blow. I was naturally very disappointed at what seemed a very unfair decision, especially having put so much effort into the tender, but I put it down to experience and got on with successfully bidding for other contracts. The following year, the client having been very dissatisfied with our competitor's performance, we were asked to re-tender for the contract. This time, we won it. We did, of course, learn some lessons from our previous failure but, most of all, we were fortunate that the individual responsible for reviewing the tenders this time was a lot more experienced.

---

11 What's the worst mistake you've made at work and how did you deal with it?

Alternative and related questions

➤ Can you tell me about a time when you made a major error at work?

The meaning behind the question

What the interviewer is trying to extract from you here is not an admission of guilt but a demonstration of how you reacted to your error and what steps you took to resolve it. You can learn a lot about someone from the way they handle mistakes.

Your answer

As with the previous question, you might think this is rather a tough one. The interviewer has specifically asked you about the worst mistake you've ever made at work. The key is to realise that everyone makes mistakes; the important thing is to learn from them and make sure you never make the same mistake twice.

Also, just because they've asked you what the worst mistake you've made was, it doesn't mean you have to tell them. Talk about a mistake that was severe but unlikely to put them off hiring you. How? By choosing carefully and placing the emphasis on what you did to resolve the situation and what you learned from the experience.

If you can subtly apportion some of the blame to circumstances out of your control, or if you can choose an example that didn't directly involve your work, then it's going to strengthen your answer. It also helps if you can pick an example which goes back some way in time. However, you definitely need to avoid coming across as someone who can't admit their own mistakes.

EXAMPLE

I think the worst mistake I ever made at work was in my first ever job, five years ago now. A more senior member of the team seemed to take an instant dislike to me from the start, and one day she was particularly unpleasant to me in front of several colleagues. Later on, I was talking to one of those colleagues who I thought was attempting to console me. Angry and hurt, I foolishly vented my feelings and told her what I thought of the person in question. I was shocked to find out that she went on to tell everyone what I had said and this certainly didn't help my relationship with the team member who was causing me problems. Rather than let the situation carry on, I chose to have a quiet word with this individual to find out what her problem was with me and to see if we could put it behind us. It turned out it was nothing personal; she just resented the fact that a friend of hers had also been interviewed for my position and had been unsuccessful. Once we had got matters out into the open, her behaviour changed and we actually got on quite well after that. However, I certainly learned a lot from the experience. I learned that careful communication is vital in managing interpersonal relationships and that if I have a problem with someone it's always best to talk it over with them rather than with someone else.

> **BLOOPER!**
>
> •
>
> Choose your example carefully. I once had a candidate tell me about the time she 'lost' a leg. She was working as a runner in an operating theatre and the surgeon handed her the limb he had just amputated. She put it down and, unfortunately, forgot all about it. 'To this day I don't really know what happened to that leg,' she reminisced wistfully.

12 How would you handle the following situation?

Alternative and related questions

> ➤ What would you do if you were presented with the following scenario?

The meaning behind the question

Often, an interviewer may pose a hypothetical, scenario-based question, telling you to imagine yourself in a difficult or negative situation and asking how you would deal with it.

By confronting you with an unexpected situation and getting you to think on your feet, they can tell a lot about how you would actually react under such circumstances.

Your answer

The answer you give will depend on the precise scenario the interviewer outlines. You need to try to identify what the expectations of you would be under the circumstances, and highlight the skills and techniques you would use to deal with the situation.

For the purposes of the example below, imagine the following scenario: You are a receptionist working at the front desk when all of a sudden an urgent email arrives, several phone lines start ringing, an important client walks in and a courier turns up with a package that requires your signature. How do you cope with this situation?

In this example, you should be able to identify that the interviewer is probing your ability to prioritise, to 'firefight' and to not panic!

My first priority would be to answer the calls whilst simultaneously presenting the waiting client and the courier with a professional and friendly smile. The calls can be answered and either put straight through or put on hold, allowing me to deal with the client and then the courier thereafter. The people waiting in front of me are able to see just how busy I am, whereas those on the phone will simply feel ignored if their calls are not answered promptly and may hang up. Having successfully prioritised the calls and the visitors, I would then be able to respond to the email when there is more time.

13 Can you tell me about a major project you have successfully completed?

Alternative and related questions

➤ Can you tell me about a major project that you have recently managed?

The meaning behind the question

The interviewer isn't really interested in the project itself, they are interested in how you successfully completed the project; looking for evidence of your ability to successfully complete a project whilst ascertaining how your key skills contribute to this ability.

Your answer

The emphasis in this question is on a project that you have *successfully* completed. It's a perfect opportunity to blow your own trumpet.

Make the most of this question to highlight your skills and abilities which led to the successful completion of the project being careful to pick those which are relevant to the job for which you are applying. Make your contribution to the project clear. What role did you play in its success?

Unless the interviewer specifically asks you about a project for which you had sole responsibility, it is reasonable to assume that they are happy with you talking about a project you worked on as part of a team, which is the case with the majority of projects.

EXAMPLE

I was recently involved in organising our participation at a trade fair. It was a major project. We'd never done a trade fair before, but we felt it could be a useful method of drumming up new business. It took a considerable amount of planning and organisation on my part. I had to assess everything that needed to be arranged in advance, from hiring the lighting set-up to liaising with our designers on the production of appropriate corporate literature for us to hand out. I had to make sure I didn't miss the smallest of details; for example, I had to check the plans of our stand to ensure our extension cables were long enough to reach all our equipment. On the day itself, we were on site very early to make sure everything was in place, tested and fully functioning prior to the arrival of the visitors just in case there were any last-minute hitches, which, thankfully, there weren't. The event was very successful and our stand attracted a lot of attention. It was a very busy day. We were able to pitch our services to hundreds of people and pass on their contact details for our sales team to follow up on. Following the success of this event, we're now looking at future events we can attend.

It is best to talk about a project you completed recently. If you go too far back, the interviewer might wonder why you can't cite a more recent example.

---

14 Can you tell me about a major problem at work that you've had to deal with?

Alternative and related questions

➤ Can you tell me about a major project you were involved with that went wrong?

The meaning behind the question

Problems are inevitable, no matter what your line of work. The interviewer isn't particularly interested in the problem per se. What they are interested in is how you dealt with it; what action you took and what the outcome was.

Employers don't want problems; they want solutions and they rely on their staff to deliver those solutions. The interviewer wants to make sure that you're just the type of employee who would be able to do that.

Your answer

This isn't the same question as question 11, 'What's the worst mistake you've made at work and how did you deal with it?', so make sure that you don't give the same answer. It would definitely be a blunder to pick an example of a problem which you yourself had caused or was caused by a colleague of yours.

Try to choose a simple, less controversial topic. The best examples to pick are those where the problem was caused by circumstances beyond your organisation's control.

Since they're referring to a problem in the past, it's important for you to choose an example which highlights your problem-solving capabilities and shows them to be relevant to the job you are applying for.

> **EXAMPLE**
>
> The weather caused us major problems just a couple of months ago. There was very heavy overnight snowfall and, with all the buses cancelled and only a few trains running, only a few members of our admin team managed to get into work. There was nothing for it but to firefight; we didn't have enough staff to get everything done that would normally need to be done. I established what our main priorities were, what activities were most essential to the running of our department and made sure that we had those covered. I identified less important tasks that we could postpone for a few days until we had the full team back. I also spoke to all the missing team members to see if there were any other urgent priorities of which we were unaware. We worked hard and fast and, despite feeling that the phone was always ringing, we managed to keep everything running smoothly until things were back to normal.

FORTY CLASSIC QUESTIONS YOU MUST BE PREPARED FOR

15 We have a problem with x. How would you resolve that?

Alternative and related questions

> ➤ Can you tell me about a difficult problem that you resolved?

> ➤ Can you tell me about a major problem at work that you've had to deal with?

The meaning behind the question

Following on from the previous question, this question is, again, directly probing your problem-solving capabilities but in a way that is directly relevant to the job for which you are applying.

The interviewer is trying to identify what you could really bring to the organisation.

The interviewer is also assessing how able you are to think on your feet because they will know there is no way you could have pre-prepared your answer to this one.

Your answer

Problem x could be just about anything. It could be a hypothetical problem but it's more likely to be a real-life problem currently facing your prospective employer.

The main difficulty you face with this question is that it's almost impossible to prepare for in advance. You're going to have to think fast. However, rather than replying immediately, I'd suggest you buy some time by getting the interviewer to talk a little more about the problem. Don't be afraid to ask a few questions first to make sure that you fully understand what the problem is and what the circumstances are. As well as arming you with more facts, this will also give you some valuable thinking time.

If you're asked the alternative question, 'Can you tell me about a difficult problem that you resolved?', then you're lucky because you can prepare a perfect example for this well in advance of the interview. Please refer to the previous question 14, 'Can you tell me about a major problem at work that you've had to deal with?', for details of how best to handle this.

16 What do you do when you disagree with your line manager?

Alternative and related questions

➤ What would you do if you disagreed with a decision taken by your line manager?

➤ Would you make your opinion known if you disagreed with a decision taken by a superior?

The meaning behind the question

Ostensibly, you might think the interviewer is testing to see how subordinate you are. This isn't really the case. It's not to an organisation's advantage to be filled with people who never question authority or who never voice their opinion. What the interviewer is really looking for is to identify the manner in which you would express your disagreement.

Your answer

A lot depends on precisely what it is that you disagree with. Is it a minor issue which boils down to a matter of your judgement against theirs or is it a more serious situation which could potentially call for your having to go over their head and discuss the matter with their superior?

You should avoid talking about the second possibility. Build your answer around the scenario of a minor disagreement and place the emphasis on how you would use your communication and interpersonal skills.

EXAMPLE

Inevitably there will be times when I disagree with my manager's point of view or with a decision she has taken or intends to take. In my current role, my manager welcomes input from her team and, whilst I appreciate that it isn't appropriate to openly disagree with her, I will query issues in private as necessary. There may be factors leading to her decision of which I am unaware. Alternatively, once we've both discussed our thoughts, we may simply agree to disagree. I have to respect that, at the end of the day, it remains her prerogative to make a decision whether I agree with it or not and to support her in that course of action to the best of my ability.

17 How would you describe yourself as a manager?

Alternative and related questions

➤ What is your management style?

➤ How do you manage people?

The meaning behind the question

There's nothing too complex about this question. The interviewer wants to know what your perception of leadership is and how you go about the day-to-day responsibility of management.

You're only going to be asked this question if you're applying for a management-level role and the interviewer is hoping to gauge just how successful you are likely to be in fulfilling such a role.

It's also going to be of interest to them to see how you perceive yourself. It can say a lot about you as a person.

Your answer

Unless you really are the perfect manager, try to interpret this question in terms of the manager you aspire to be because that's the kind of manager the interviewer is wanting you to be.

There are two main aspects to a management role.

➤ Getting the job done.

➤ Handling the people who will help you to get the job done.

Your answer needs to cover both of these.

The precise points you raise in your answer will depend on the kind of management role for which you are applying. Different employers will have different expectations of how their managers should behave and what they are expected to achieve.

Here are my ten top tips for effectively handling and managing your subordinates:

➤ Develop good working relationships with your subordinates but be wary of becoming too emotionally close. It can weaken and undermine your authority.

- Be fair. Treat your subordinates all equally and objectively. Avoid having favourites. And treat them all as you would wish to be treated yourself.

- Be prepared to put on your cross face and to take appropriate measures with those who fail to perform to the required standards. But use it sparingly!

- Praise in public; criticise in private. Never humiliate a subordinate. You want them on your side, not working against you.

- Don't lose your temper and never yell and shout. It just makes you look weak, foolish and out of control.

- Demonstrate empathy and the ability to understand their individual points of view. Make them feel understood and their opinions recognised.

- Demand the best of people that they can achieve but be aware of their limitations and don't make excessive demands; it's counterproductive.

- If a subordinate comes to you for help, give them the time and attention they deserve. It's your job to help them and to teach them how to help themselves.

- Remember that you're not God. You don't know it all. A little humility and a little less arrogance will only increase your subordinates' opinion of you.

- You'll most likely be somebody else's subordinate. Don't hesitate to seek their advice or intervention if you are worried about how to handle a situation.

BLOOPER!

'I don't do anything that I can make someone else do for me!'

I'm a very hands-on manager. Whilst I am clearly in charge of my team, we are nonetheless a team and I am very much a member of that team. When the circumstances require it, I will assert my authority and lead my staff in the direction I have determined we should go. However, I'm always open to input ideas and suggestions and consider myself to be very approachable in that respect. I realise the importance of motivating my staff to deliver their best and I'm tactful and diplomatic when dealing with potential problems; I believe a lot more can be achieved through communication than through conflict. I am nevertheless very results driven and expect every member of my team to pull their weight and help us to achieve our common goals.

18 Can you give me an example of when you have successfully coached a member of your team?

Alternative and related questions

➤ Have you ever been asked to help train a new member of staff?

The meaning behind the question

You'd be wrong in thinking that this is a question just for managers. This question could be asked of anyone who works in a team, which is pretty much everyone. In all lines of work the ability to help others to further develop their skills and experience is a valuable attribute. How you describe your example will tell the interviewer a lot about you.

Your answer

You need to structure your answer logically to identify what the circumstances were, why the individual needed coaching, how you went about coaching them and, most important of all, what the outcome was. Coaching a team member is a project like any other. In order to deliver a successful answer to this question you need to demonstrate a successful outcome.

The example you select will depend on your own personal experiences but, whatever example you choose, make sure you come out of it as the hero of the day.

If you're struggling to find an example, then the easiest thing to do is pick a time when you had to help deal with a new member of staff. Coaching is a very broad term and helping to train a new colleague certainly falls under its umbrella.

EXAMPLE

In my current job for a mail-order company, I work as part of a team processing orders received and liaising directly with our customers by telephone to handle and resolve any problems or queries. Whilst administration forms the majority of the workload, there's also a lot of customer contact. Recently, my manager took the decision to hire a new team member who had a lot of very valuable customer-facing experience but not so much administrative experience. Whilst the new member of staff clearly needed no help dealing with customers on the telephone, it was obvious from the start that she was struggling with the administrative side of things. As I was one of the most experienced members of the team, my manager asked if I could take this person under my wing and help her to resolve the administrative difficulties she was having. Over a period of several days I took the time for her to initially shadow me in the work I was doing, before moving on to let her do the work under my careful observation. She learned very quickly and within the week she was fully up to scratch and has since become an invaluable member of the team.

---

19 What is your customer service philosophy?

Alternative and related questions

➤ Can you tell me about a difficult client/customer you've had and how you handled them?

➤ Can you give me an example of an occasion when you exceeded a client's/customer's expectations?

The meaning behind the question

Most organisations provide a product or service to a customer. Some definitions of customer are obvious: Marks & Spencer sells sandwiches to the public. Some are less obvious: JobcentrePlus helps the unemployed return to work.

Customer service skills are important in many different walks of life and this question is designed to probe your customer service skills. It is more far-reaching than that, though, because many of the same skills which will enable an individual to work well with customers will also help them to work well with their colleagues.

Your answer

However the interviewer phrases the question, the main thrust of your answer should be to outline your customer service skills.

If you can illustrate your answer with an example of when you have delivered outstanding customer service, then so much the better. Outstanding customer service could include resolving a difficult client's complaint or it could be a case of your having exceeded a customer's expectations. Whatever example you select, make sure it is one which shows you in a positive light, i.e. if you want to talk about an unhappy client; it had better not be your actions which caused the dissatisfaction!

EXAMPLE

I believe the customer is central to everything we do. Profits are certainly our ultimate goal but, without customer satisfaction, profits will suffer. I attach a lot of importance to customer service. A business is nothing without its customers and it's vital to recognise this. I believe I have strong customer service skills, and working with the public is certainly something I enjoy. It's not always easy, of course. Recently, I had to deal with a particularly difficult client who was – fairly unreasonably, it has to be said – very dissatisfied with the solution our sales team had sold them. Rather than let the complaint escalate, I took the time to calmly and patiently listen to the customer and to demonstrate that I understood and empathised with their concerns. This alone took a lot of the wind out of their sails. I went on to give them my viewpoint, addressing their concerns one by one and explaining why I felt the solution they had been sold was the best one for them. It turned out that they had misunderstood what was being offered and, once realisation set in, they were actually quite apologetic!

20 How did you get your last job?

Alternative and related questions

➤ How did you locate your last job?

The meaning behind the question

This is a surprisingly popular question among interviewers. The reason is that, whilst seemingly a very simple little question, your answer can give the interviewer insight into numerous different areas. It can help them to assess how much initiative you have, how determined and tenacious you are, how driven you are and how much you plan and control your own career.

Your answer

There are two different ways of interpreting this question, so you need to make sure you cover both bases. First is the question of how you actually managed to locate your last job (recruitment agency, network contact, speculative application, headhunted etc.). Then there is the question of how you went about securing the job – how you convinced the employer that you were the right person for the job. You need to aim to portray an image of somebody in control of their own destiny – not someone who just goes with the flow.

EXAMPLE

It was actually quite complicated. I was keen for a new challenge and had already started looking when I saw in the local newspaper that they were opening a new branch in the area. I sent in a speculative application to the HR department at their head office and they wrote back to say that they would only be recruiting through their preferred recruitment agency. So I called them up immediately and, having run through a few key points on my CV, managed to persuade them to at least interview me. They also interviewed a spread of candidates from the recruitment agency but, after a second interview and then a third interview with the marketing director, I was ultimately offered the job.

21 What does your current job involve on a day-to-day basis?

Alternative and related questions

➤ Can you describe an average day in your job?

The meaning behind the question

They've read your CV; they know what your job involves. Now they want to hear it straight from the horse's mouth. There's nothing more to their question than that but giving the best answer is a little more complicated.

Your answer

As I said, the interviewer has read your CV (or application form) so they know more or less what your job entails. It would definitely be a mistake to answer this question by simply reeling off in detail everything you've already stated on your CV. The last thing you want to do is bore the interviewer.

EXAMPLE

My most important responsibility is to achieve sales. I spend most of my day on the shop floor, talking directly to potential customers and trying to establish their needs. I have a very thorough knowledge of our product range so, if they're unsure of their decision, I can give them appropriate advice. I can also steer them towards other, perhaps more expensive product lines that they haven't already considered. By building rapport with the customer and addressing any concerns they may have I have a good chance of closing the sale. I also aim to up-sell on the till where possible, to maximise the value of each new customer. Amongst other responsibilities, I help to control stock levels and liaise with head office accordingly to make sure we are neither overstocked nor understocked. I am also involved in the financial management of the branch, working alongside the branch manager to put together monthly reports etc. Given my level of experience, I am also tasked with helping to bring on board new members of staff, training them in our systems and helping them to maximise their sales potential.

Whilst the description you give on your CV will be comprehensive (and rightly so), when it comes to answering this question you'd do better to skip a lot of the detail and focus on what's really important – what your job is really about. In particular, you want to focus on areas of your current job which most closely match the job for which you are now applying.

Rather than phrasing your work in terms of duties, try to portray what you do in terms of responsibilities.

22 What contribution do you make to the department in which you work?

Alternative and related questions

➤ How does your job relate to the overall goals of your department/ organisation?

The meaning behind the question

The interviewer could have rephrased this question: 'Are you able to see the bigger picture?' They are searching for evidence that you understand the purpose and goals of your department as a whole and how your role fits into the big scheme of things. Whilst it might not be vital to your ability to undertake your job, it is always preferable for an employee to understand what the overall purpose is of their team or department and what part they are expected to play in that.

Your answer

Even if the interviewer hasn't phrased the question using the word contribution, you still need to place a clear emphasis in your answer on what it is that you contribute to the overall goals of your department. You've got to demonstrate your value. The interviewer knows what job you perform, but how is it of benefit to your colleagues and to your employer?

Some people won't necessarily work in a specific department as such but if this is the case for you, then you can simply talk about the contribution you make to other departments and to the organisation as a whole as in the example below.

EXAMPLE

Whilst I am technically part of the IT department, all my colleagues focus very much on keeping the company's computer infrastructure fully functional. However, as the company's only Web developer, I work very much on my own in managing and enhancing the website. I do liaise closely with other departments particularly marketing and HR. As the website is primarily used as a marketing vehicle and as a way to source new employees, my work is of significant importance to both of these departments. The systems I put in place to collect potential sales leads online make a major contribution to the results of the sales team; these days more and more of our new business comes via the website. And, by identifying ways to attract potential new employees online, I have contributed to a reduction in the amount we spend on recruitment consultants, again resulting in a direct impact on the company's bottom line.

23 What changes have you made to your current job role since you started?

Alternative and related questions

➤ How have you changed the job you've been doing?

The meaning behind the question

All job roles evolve over time – some more than others. The interviewer isn't asking how your job has changed since you were first appointed; they are asking how *you* have changed it. They're looking for evidence of initiative, drive and enthusiasm. The best employees are always looking for ways to make improvements; to change things for the better. It's all too easy for an employee to sit back and just accept things the way they are but that's not the type of employee who is going to help drive an organisation forward.

Your answer

An interviewer should only be asking this question if your current job is one in which you can reasonably be expected to have made changes to your role.

In many roles there is limited scope for making changes, so your interviewer probably won't be expecting too dramatic an example. If you have been responsible for a tangible improvement to your role, then this is obviously going to be an excellent choice. Alternatively, it should be more than sufficient to describe ways in which you took on additional duties and responsibilities that weren't part of your original job description.

Be aware that this is the type of question that an interviewer is particularly likely to check up on when taking up your references, so it's essential to be absolutely honest.

Word of warning

For some reason, candidates are particularly prone to misunderstanding this question and interpreting it along the lines of 'What changes have you made in your current job?' This is a very different question and, no matter how good your answer to this question, your interviewer won't be impressed if you fail to answer the question they actually asked.

EXAMPLE

When I first took over the role, I noticed that my predecessor (who was in the job for many years) had been using a number of rather outdated and laborious systems to help him manage the allocation of work to our subcontractors. This was clearly wasting a significant amount of time – and time is money. I consulted with my manager and outlined a proposal to scrap these various manual systems and replace them with a single system running on software I had become adept at using in my previous role. Given the low cost of the software and the obvious advantages of my proposal, my manager agreed to the plan. Having spent a couple of weeks setting up the new system, I reduced my workload substantially and I was able to use this spare time to help my manager with his financial reporting. This gave me useful, additional experience and also freed up my manager to spend more time on other issues.

24 What have you learned in your last job?

Alternative and related questions

➤ What have you learned in each of your previous roles?

The meaning behind the question

The interviewer could have asked 'What did you learn in your last job that will be of use to you in this job?' because that is what they are driving at. They are not asking you to talk about your duties, responsibilities or achievements. They are specifically asking in what ways you developed professionally whilst working in your last job (or any particular job of their choice).

Your answer

It's vital that your answer should cite one or more examples which are directly relevant to the role for which you are now applying. There's no point in discussing something which isn't going to be of obvious value to you – or, more specifically, your employer – in your next job.

The chances are that your previous role(s) will have prepared you in various ways to meet the challenge of your next job. Try to ascertain what is likely to be of most interest to the interviewer. What are the key requirements of this vacancy? What have you learned that will ensure you meet those requirements? Select at least one – if not two or three – ideas and turn them into strong selling points.

EXAMPLE

My last job was an excellent learning opportunity and I developed my skills and experience in numerous different ways. Whilst I already had strong IT skills, I didn't have any previous experience of Microsoft Access. When my employer introduced a new order management system which used Access, I was given the opportunity to undertake additional training, to be able to work effectively with this. I was then able to put this training into practice on a day-to-day basis, and I am now extremely adept at using the package. I also learned a great deal about handling customers. My previous roles were not customer facing, so it was great to have the chance to develop this area of my experience.

There's no need to highlight how this relates to the role you're applying for. It should be self-evident and, if you make a point of it, there is a risk the interviewer might think you're just saying what they want to hear.

25 Can you tell me about your last appraisal?

Alternative and related questions

➤ How was your performance rated in your last appraisal?

➤ How would you comment on your last appraisal?

➤ What areas for improvement were identified at your last appraisal?

The meaning behind the question

Appraisals are supposed to address both your strengths and your weaknesses; both your achievements and your failings. However, the interviewer will know that appraisals focus more on where there is room for improvement than on giving you a pat on the back. This question is a clever ploy to get you to confess precisely where there is room for improvement in your performance.

Your answer

You're going to need to be careful with your answer to this question. For a start, it's very important to be totally honest because the interviewer can easily check up on this sort of information when taking up your references and, if it's an internal vacancy for which you are applying, then you can be more or less sure they will already have examined your last appraisal.

It's not a difficult question to get right. You need to focus on the positive points that were brought up in your last appraisal and only touch briefly on any less positive points; making sure you confirm these are issues you have now addressed or are in the process of addressing. You're under no obligation to relate every last detail of your last appraisal, so I would vote in favour of mentioning several positive points but limiting your answer to cover just one weaker point. If your appraisal brought up an apparent weak point that you can put a positive slant on, then so much the better.

Not all employers have a formal appraisal system and this will certainly simplify your answer! It would, however, be a good idea to mention that, whilst there was no formal system in place, you have routinely received positive feedback on your performance, both from your boss and from your colleagues.

EXAMPLE

My last appraisal was very positive. My manager felt that I had made excellent progress in many areas and had really mastered the intricacies of the project we were working on. He did say that he felt other members of the team had become too dependent on me and that a lot of my time was being taken up in showing them how to tackle difficult or unusual issues. Whilst he perceived this as an area for improvement, I perceived this as further evidence that the time is now right for me to take a step up to a management-level position hence my applying for this role with yourselves.

---

26 How would you describe your current boss?

Alternative and related questions

➤ What do you think of your current boss?

➤ What kind of relationship do you have with your current boss?

The meaning behind the question

The interviewer may just be idly curious as to what your current boss is like, but don't count on it. They are much more likely to be probing your perceptions of authority and, in particular, how you handle authority. Whilst seemingly innocuous, this is actually quite a loaded question. If the interviewer identifies you as having any problems with authority, then it's going to be a big black mark on your application.

Your answer

Regardless of what a loser you might think your boss is, it isn't going to get you anywhere to slate them. You should most certainly avoid making any disparaging comments. Statistically, having problems with their boss is the number one reason people give for changing jobs. However, you'd do well just to give a reasonably complimentary description and portray a positive working relationship between the two of you.

EXAMPLE

I'm fortunate to have a pretty positive working relationship with my boss. She gives me a high degree of latitude to get on with my job whilst always being there to help me with any unusual or difficult situations and lend me the benefit of her experience. Like many managers, she's often very busy but she does a good job of closely supervising her team, steering us in the right direction and helping us to achieve the results that are expected of us. I know she appreciates the work I do and this obviously helps to motivate me and make me to strive to achieve my very best.

27 Why did you leave that job?

Alternative and related questions

➤ Have you ever been made redundant and, if so, why?
➤ Have you ever been fired?

The meaning behind the question

This question is distinct from 'Why do you wish to leave your current position?' that we covered in the previous chapter in that it's not exploring your current motivators in changing jobs; it's exploring your reasons for having left a job.

The interviewer might also be hoping to turn up any skeletons you may have in your cupboard; for example, dismissals.

Your answer

We've already covered the topic of changing jobs in detail in the previous chapter under 'Why do you wish to leave your current position?' Much of that advice will apply to this question. However, here I'd like to focus on two special cases: two more negative reasons why you might have left a previous job.

➤ Being made redundant

➤ Being fired/sacked

I would immediately like to apologise to any readers who have been made redundant. It is not my intention to cause any offence by listing redundancy as a negative reason for leaving a job. I fully appreciate that redundancy is a difficult time and that there's often little justice in an employer's choice of who to make redundant. I empathise entirely. However, my reason for including it in this list is not to suggest you've been made redundant through any fault of your own but because having been made redundant may unfortunately be perceived in a negative fashion by a prospective employer. It is, therefore, a hurdle you need to deal with and which I will show you how to deal with.

Redundancy hurts. There are no two ways about it. However, you must conceal any bitterness and resentment you may feel and convey to the interviewer that 'such is life', 'these things happen', it wasn't your fault. It is the position that is redundant, not the individual person. Under no circumstances should you criticise the employer that laid you off. Rather than dwell on negative aspects, you must aim to emphasise any positive outcomes; for example, it gave you the opportunity to undertake some valuable training or that it meant you were able to move on to a new and better position.

EXAMPLE

Unfortunately, a major client, that my department was responsible for supplying, decided to withdraw completely from the UK and close all their branches. It appears they had overreached themselves in deciding to expand beyond the USA. Almost everyone in my department was subsequently made redundant. However, with hindsight, it all worked out very well in the end because I was able to secure a new – and more senior – position within just a couple of months.

If you've been fired from a previous role, then this is a tough one to deal with; it's hard to put a positive slant on such matters.

There are two points I need to make about how you should handle this. Firstly, you must be truthful; it's easy for a prospective employer to check these sorts of detail. Secondly, you must convey the circumstances as calmly and dispassionately as possible, acknowledge responsibility for the causes of your dismissal and, above all else, convince the interviewer that you learned a great deal from the experience and that this will never, ever happen again.

There are various words and expressions which can be used to describe being dismissed from a job, such as 'sacked' and 'fired'. However, these have more negative connotations than simply saying you were dismissed. You should avoid using them in your answer.

EXAMPLE

I was only in that job for a couple of months and I unfortunately left it sooner than I would have liked to. I had an initial probationary period of three months and, during that time I regrettably had an argument with a customer. I felt they were being extremely unreasonable and, rather than pacifying them, I let the situation escalate. It turned out that they were a long-standing customer and they used their influence to insist that my manager dismiss me. I was young and inexperienced and I learnt a great deal from this. I would certainly never argue with a customer again; I know that there are much better ways to resolve such a situation.

BLOOPER!

It's probably a good idea to avoid the following answer given by one candidate: 'The company made me a scapegoat, just like my three previous employers!'

28 Which of your jobs was the best?

Alternative and related questions

➤ What's the best job you have ever had?

➤ Can you describe the best job you have ever had?

➤ How would you define your dream job?

➤ In which job were you the happiest/most fulfilled?

The meaning behind the question

This is potentially a trick question. Does the interviewer really care which of your jobs was best? Or are they more interested in identifying what your conception of the perfect job is and how that matches or differs from the vacancy for which they are currently interviewing you? It's much more likely to be the latter. By identifying what you have most enjoyed in the past they can assess how likely you are to enjoy this job in the future.

Your answer

You should endeavour to pick a job that is not greatly dissimilar from the one for which you are applying. You then need to explain your choice in such a way as to emphasise the similarities between that role and this current vacancy – subtly, of course.

EXAMPLE

I have tried to plan my career path carefully, only changing jobs when the right role presented itself. However, I would say my best ever job was my role with Elisabeth Elkins Catering. I was given a considerable degree of autonomy to conceive, plan and implement our marketing strategy. I had a highly productive working relationship with the managing director and the outcome was clearly very successful, our sales had more than tripled by the end of my two years.

Word of warning

Avoid citing your current job. The interviewer will wonder:

➤ If it's that great then why do you really want to leave?

➤ If they do give you this job, is there a risk you might later regret it?

29 Why is there a gap in your CV?

Alternative and related questions

➤ What did you do during this gap in your employment?

➤ Can you tell me more about this break in your career history?

The meaning behind the question

There are two elements here:

➤ The interviewer will be interested in the reasons for there being a gap in your CV; why you experienced a period of unemployment.

➤ They will also be interested in what you did during that period of unemployment.

Your answer

Most people have a gap or two in their career history. It's very common and not normally anything to worry about. There is, however, only one explanation that an employer is really going to view favourably:

➤ Further training/education.

Other common – and conceivably constructive – reasons include:

➤ Raising a child

➤ Caring for another dependant

➤ Travel

But there are also reasons which will definitely be viewed negatively:

➤ Inability to find a suitable position

➤ Ill health

➤ Imprisonment

If the reason for the gap in your career history isn't obviously negative, then there shouldn't be a gap in your CV. You should include a brief entry explaining the situation. This will prevent an interviewer from asking you, 'Why is there a gap in your CV?' and will instead prompt them to ask the more positive question, 'Can you tell me more about this break in your career history?'

Further training/education: This is very simple and should already be covered within your CV but maybe the interviewer has missed it. You need to simply politely draw their attention to the further training/education you undertook and use this as an opportunity to talk about why you chose this option and how it adds value to your application.

Raising a child/caring for another dependant: If you took time out of your career in order to care for a family member or close friend, then it is very much your own private affair but one that an interviewer should hopefully view favourably. You should have included a brief entry in your CV explaining the circumstances and the interviewer should refrain from probing too deeply into the matter. The same applies for time out to raise your own family. I suggest you refer to the section on sexual discrimination in the next chapter, Chapter 21: Illegal questions – and how to dodge them, so that you are fully aware of your rights in this respect.

Travel: Taking a sabbatical to go travelling is often seen by an employer as a positive thing. Many will believe that the cultural awareness and sense of independence you will have gained as a result of the experience will prove to be of value to them. Also, if you've already taken time out to travel, then it means you're less likely to suddenly disappear to travel the world just as they've got you settled in. This is a common worry among employers, particularly when it comes to younger employees. If you're questioned on this then it is important to emphasise that it was something you 'needed to do' and now you've 'got it out of your system'. You may also be able to make reference to any temporary and part-time work you undertook in other countries if that could be an additional selling point for you.

Unfortunately, general unemployment and ill health are unlikely – at least initially – to be viewed favourably by an interviewer. And imprisonment certainly won't be viewed favourably.

Inability to find a suitable position: This is definitely the most common cause for there being a gap in a CV. The problem you face is that if you tell an interviewer you were struggling to find work, then that's inevitably going to worry them. You need to deal with this by explaining carefully that the right job isn't always available at the right time.

Ill health: If you have been absent from work as a result of a significant illness or a major accident, then the interviewer should appreciate that these things do happen.

Imprisonment: This is always going to be an extremely difficult issue to handle and I would suggest you refer to the detailed section on criminal convictions in the next chapter, Chapter 21: Illegal questions – and how to dodge them.

30 What do you know about us as an organisation?

Alternative and related questions

> What is your impression of our organisation?

> Why do you want to work for this organisation?

The meaning behind the question

Remember the candidate I mentioned earlier who, upon being asked what he could bring to the company, responded with 'What is it that you do again?'?

The interviewer wants to make sure you've done your homework, that you really understand what their organisation is all about and that you have a realistic expectation of what it would be like to work for such an organisation. Whilst they're not going to be deliberately fishing for compliments they will want to ensure that you do have a positive impression of their organisation. Why do you want to work for them in particular?

Your answer

In the previous chapter we covered the closely related question, 'Why do you want to work for this organisation?' The difference with this question is the greater emphasis you need to place on what you know about the organisation rather than why you want to work for their organisation in particular.

Spell out to the interviewer the key points you know about their organisation and how you come to know them; for example, because you've researched their website, or you've read about them in the newspaper. But don't go into excessive detail.

Make sure that you put a positive spin on any points you raise and, if at all possible, communicate how you feel you are well suited to working for such an organisation.

Avoid saying anything negative or bringing up any bad press etc. that the organisation may have had.

EXAMPLE

I've done some research into your organisation to ensure that I fully understand what kind of organisation I would be working for. I read on your website that your sales levels have grown at an average of 25 per cent year on year for the past five years and that you are now working on your expansion into the United States. You're clearly a very progressive organisation and that's exactly what I'm looking for. I want to work for an organisation which doesn't stand still, which is expanding and taking on new and interesting challenges. I've also read a lot of customer comments on various third-party websites and the quality of your service is clearly very impressive.

---

31 What do you know about our products/services?

Alternative and related questions

➤ Have you ever bought our products/used our services?

The meaning behind the question

The interviewer is again testing to see how interested you really are in the vacancy as defined by the amount of time you have spent research-ing the operation. Some roles will, of course, require greater product/service knowledge than others and, if you are applying for a role where such knowledge is critical, for example, sales, then the question will take on another dimension. If you can't prove that you fully understand the product/service that the company supplies, then how can you hope to be able to sell it?

Your answer

If you've prepared properly for your interview, then you should be able to demonstrate a reasonably in-depth understanding of the organisation's products/services. The degree to which this will be important will depend on your precise line of work. As well as conveying basic facts, it is also a good idea to provide a gentle critique. Whilst you should aim to be more complimentary than critical, if you are able to identify areas for improvement, ideally areas which you yourself would be able to improve, then it is likely to impress the interviewer and count very much in your favour. The best employees rarely accept the status quo; they are always looking for ways to improve things.

EXAMPLE

I've actually got one of your posters framed on the wall at home. I was already familiar with the range you offer, and since seeing this vacancy advertised I have had a closer and more detailed look. I'm naturally impressed by what I've seen. They're printed to a high degree of quality, something that isn't always the case with posters produced by other companies and yet they remain very reasonably priced. Whilst you certainly have many interesting and commercially appealing designs, I do feel that some parts of the range are becoming a little dated. I would certainly welcome the challenge not only of revamping existing designs within the range but also of further developing the range in new and interesting directions.

---

32 What do you think are our organisation's greatest strengths, weaknesses, opportunities and threats?

Alternative and related questions

➤ What do you think is the greatest advantage we have over the competition?

The meaning behind the question

This is a complex question. The interviewer wants to put your knowledge of their organisation – and of the market in general – to the test. Their secondary objective will be to see how you handle a question in four parts: strengths, weaknesses, opportunities and threats. Questions which are really three or four questions in one are often considered to be good basic indicators of Intelligence, showing how well your brain can absorb, hold and process multiple concepts simultaneously. Trust me; this is not an easy question especially when you are already under pressure.

Your answer

Fear not. Tricky as this question is, if you've prepared for it (which, if you're reading this, you hopefully will have done), then it all boils down to keeping your cool, breaking the question down into its component parts and addressing each of them in turn. You should also aim to go heavy on the strengths and opportunities, and a little more gently with the weaknesses and threats. It's a big question but try to keep your answer reasonably concise. As with other questions about potentially negative issues, try to put a positive spin on matters. If the role you are being interviewed for could play a part in tackling these weaknesses and threats, then make sure you say so.

EXAMPLE

I think your greatest strengths are your market-leading position and the customer service philosophy which has resulted in this. Every business has its weakness and I think we'd agree that your greatest weakness is the lack of a comprehensive marketing strategy. As we've already discussed, you focus on a few key marketing avenues and are leaving a lot of money on the table in certain other areas. I firmly believe this is something I can help you with and that the development of a broad and consistent marketing strategy is also your greatest opportunity. I also feel that expanding internationally represents another major opportunity. As for threats, the greatest threat is quite simply the competition. It's vitally important for you to continue to stay one step ahead of them.

33 What do you know about the vacancy for which you are applying?

Alternative and related questions

➤ Why have you applied for this vacancy?

➤ What appeals to you most about this vacancy?

The meaning behind the question

The interviewer wants to make sure that you really understand the role for which you are applying, and that you fully appreciate what would be involved if you were to be appointed to the role. If you haven't been questioned separately about this, then they will also be trying to glean why it is that you applied for this vacancy and why it appeals to you.

Your answer

Clearly, if you don't have a reasonably thorough understanding of the role (from the job description or person specification etc.), then you shouldn't even be at the interview. You need to demonstrate comprehensively to the interviewer that you fully appreciate what the role entails and, ideally, you want to try to pre-empt the next question in this chapter, question 34, 'How do your skills and experience match the job description/person specification?'

For advice on how to deal with explaining why it is that you have applied for this vacancy and why it appeals to you, please refer to the separate questions, 'Why have you applied for this vacancy?' in the previous chapter and question 35, 'What appeals to you most about this vacancy?'

EXAMPLE

I've carefully studied both the job description and the person specification so I believe I'm fully aware of the precise duties and responsibilities the role entails. You've also helped to clarify a few points during the course of this interview.

You can then go on to deliver your prepared answer to the following question.

34 How do your skills and experience match the job description/person specification?

Alternative and related questions

➤ Do you feel your skills and experience match the job description/ person specification?

➤ Do you feel that you have the skills and experience necessary to undertake this job?

The meaning behind the question

Answering this question is going to be one of your interviewer's primary goals. Many of the other questions will lead them towards an answer but sometimes the interviewer will just come out and ask you directly to tell them how you match the job description/person specification.

As well as helping the interviewer to gauge how well your skills and experience match what they are looking for, this question will also reveal a lot about how you perceive the job in question.

Your answer

You're not going to get away with answering, 'Very well!' to this question. What the interviewer expects you to do – and what you very much need to do – is to explain precisely *how* your skills and experience match the job description/person specification.

Job descriptions and person specifications are often very lengthy and comprehensive. You don't want to go into too much detail when answering this question – not least because it could get rather boring! The best strategy to adopt is for you to select a handful of issues and briefly talk about each in turn expressing each in terms of your prospective employer's needs.

Naturally, you will need to give this some thought and to have determined in advance what skills and experience the interviewer is going to be most interested in.

I believe my skills and experience is a very good match for the person specification. You're looking for someone with a significant amount of high-level experience in the retail clothing sector. I now have 25 years' experience within this sector, most recently as general manager of a flagship central London store. You need someone with considerable skill in financial management, able to build turnover – and, most importantly, to build turnover profitably. In my current role my branch now has an annual turnover of £5 million – 40 per cent higher than when I took over the role three years ago. Our profit margin has also grown – from 10 per cent to 15 per cent, meaning that profits have more than doubled in just the last three years. The role demands an individual who is adept at managing and leading a large team; I'm currently responsible for 65 retail staff. The role also requires an individual who is able to build profitable long-term relationships with key, high-value clients. Successfully catering to the needs of VIP clients is essential to my current role and certainly an aspect that I very much enjoy. Overall, I feel I'm a very good match for the job but would of course be delighted to discuss any particular points in greater detail if you wish.

This answer has obviously been written from the point of view of someone seeking a very senior role. However, the basic principles can easily be adapted to your own specific circumstances. Remember that my examples are purely intended to help illustrate the points made; it's essential for you to think for yourself and to create your own answers.

35 What appeals to you most about this vacancy?

Alternative and related questions

➤ What are you most looking forward to in this job?

➤ What is it that you are looking for in a new job?

➤ Why have you applied for this vacancy?

The meaning behind the question

This question is similar to the question, 'Why have you applied for this vacancy?' that we discussed in the previous chapter. However, it is sufficiently different – and sufficiently popular – to warrant covering it separately.

The interviewer knows that there will be a number of factors which draw you to this vacancy. What they are looking for with this question is to identify your key motivator – what really matters most to you. This will naturally give some insight into you as both a professional and a person.

Your answer

There's a right way and a wrong way to answer this question. The wrong way is to see matters entirely from your own point of view and to cite some aspect of the vacancy which meets your own needs first and foremost. The right way is to make sure you identify some aspect of the vacancy which you can talk about in such a way as to place emphasis on how you meet the organisation's needs. The interviewer is more interested in how you meet the company's needs than in how they can meet yours.

EXAMPLE

I'm particularly taken with the importance you place on customer service. In too many organisations customer service is very much a secondary priority, whereas you place the customer at the centre of everything you do. As a customer service manager, I am naturally very committed to excellence in customer service, and I am very keen to work with an organisation that attaches the same importance to customer service that I do. A business is nothing without its customers; it's vital to recognise this, and your reputation for customer service is clearly enviable. It sets you apart from the competition.

---

36 Why have you chosen this line of work?

Alternative and related questions

➤ What took you into this line of work?

➤ What do you like best about this line of work?

The meaning behind the question

The interviewer could have asked, 'Was it the right choice?' because this is what they are trying to establish, was this the right choice for you and, if so, why? As with almost every other question, the interviewer will be looking for ways in which your answer can be applied to the requirements of the job for which you are applying.

Your answer

Hopefully you've already gone a long way towards convincing the interviewer that you want this job. Now you need to convince them that this line of work really is the right one for you. In what ways are you best suited to it?

You definitely need to demonstrate enthusiasm for your work and if you can manage to demonstrate passion then that's even better. Above all you need to show an interest in your line of work and give sound reasons for your having embarked upon this particular career path. Avoid at all costs giving the impression that it is something you just randomly drifted into.

Try to sprinkle your explanation with specific examples of relevant skills and abilities.

EXAMPLE

Both my parents are accountants, so I grew up listening to them talking about their work, and I was always very interested in their working lives. Whilst I considered a range of other options, I've always had a particular talent for mathematics and, ultimately, accountancy was the best choice. I enjoy working with figures; I enjoy applying my mathematical abilities to real-world problems. I also enjoy working with others and find it very rewarding to get to grips with a client's precise circumstances and then help them to find the best solutions to the financial problems they are facing. Accountancy was without doubt the right choice for me.

37 Are there any other organisations to which you are applying?

Alternative and related questions

➤ What other organisations are you applying to?

➤ What other jobs have you applied for?

➤ Have you had any other interviews yet?

➤ Have you received any job offers yet?

The meaning behind the question

This question has nothing directly to do with your ability to do the job. The interviewer is trying to gauge how important this particular application is to you and how much you are in demand with other – possibly competing – organisations. They want to assess how discerning you are or, the other side of the coin, how desperate you are. If you've already received a firm offer from another organisation, then they will know they need to act fast if they don't want to lose you.

Your answer

You've got to tread carefully here. You don't want to be trapped into disclosing too much detail especially the names of specific organisations. The only exception to this is if you are also applying to a direct competitor. It's a risky move, the interviewer might see this as rather mercenary on your part but it can motivate them to want to secure your services rather than let 'the enemy' acquire you. Generally, it's best to dodge the question somewhat and give an appropriately vague answer but, above all, to be truthful. If you round off your answer by emphasising that this particular vacancy is your preferred choice, then the interviewer is unlikely to press you for further details of your other applications.

EXAMPLE

Finding the right position is obviously very important to me, so I am being rather thorough in my job search. I have been quite selective, but I have identified a number of different jobs and organisations which fit my criteria and my applications for these vacancies have reached varying stages. However, this opportunity with yourselves remains my preferred choice because of the specifics of the role in question and because the organisation itself is one I feel to be particularly appropriate to me.

38 How does this job compare to others for which you are applying?

Alternative and related questions

➤ Why do you want this particular job?

➤ What most attracts you to this opportunity rather than other vacancies you have applied for?

The meaning behind the question

This is clearly a more probing question than the previous question and you may well find it being asked as a follow-up to that question. The interviewer is trying to gauge how motivated you are to win this particular role as opposed to one of the others currently open to you. They want to know where they fit on the scale.

Your answer

You're going to have to tread a fine line here. It's vital to communicate that this job is, of course, your preferred choice (even if one of the other offers is blatantly superior). However, you most certainly don't want to give the impression that this job is your *only* choice. That would severely weaken your position. The best strategy is to sidestep the question as best you can and focus very much on the vacancy at hand and what most attracts you to this job and to this organisation.

This job clearly has the edge on other applications I am pursuing. I have taken my time to identify a number of possibilities which are closely suited to me so as not to waste my time or anybody else's. They all have various pros and cons, but I am particularly attracted to this job because I feel it offers the best opportunities for me to develop professionally and make a major contribution. It's a perfect match for my skills and experience. I also believe I will fit in very well with the organisation as a whole.

39 Can you describe your ideal employer to me?

Alternative and related questions

➤ Which of your employers was the best?

The meaning behind the question

By identifying what you perceive as the perfect employer, the interviewer can assess how closely their organisation fits this profile and how well you are likely to fit in with the organisation. It's a clever question and sets a trap that a weaker candidate is likely to walk straight into. If they don't fit your definition of the ideal employer, then why would they want to hire you?

Your answer

It doesn't really matter what your idea of an ideal employer is. What matters is that your description should match the organisation to which you are now applying. Of course, if there's a big difference between your prospective employer and your conception of the ideal employer then you should perhaps be asking yourself whether this is really going to be the right job for you.

The easiest way to tackle this question is to first identify what it is that you like best about your prospective employer and then build your description of your ideal employer around this.

If you've already prepared an answer to 'Why do you want to work for this organisation?' (which I covered in the previous chapter), then you can recycle some of the ideas you had for that.

> **EXAMPLE**
>
> My ideal employer would be a large yet growing company with a strong reputation within its sector, a company which offers plenty of scope for progression within the hierarchy. Whilst my preference is for a larger organisation, I want to work for a company which nevertheless has a dynamic and progressive approach. Your organisation certainly more than meets those requirements.

Word of warning

It would be inappropriate to openly state that you feel their organisation to be the 'perfect' employer. You will inevitably come across as phoney!

40 What sort of person would you most like to work for?

Alternative and related questions

> ➤ Can you tell me about the best boss you've ever had?
> ➤ Putting yourself in your manager's shoes, what is the best way to manage you?

The meaning behind the question

Along the same lines as the previous question, the interviewer is looking to identify how well you are likely to fit in with your manager. If your prospective manager differs significantly from the description you give, then it's going to raise questions in the interviewer's mind as to how well you are likely to be able to work together.

You should also be aware that the way you answer this question can reveal a lot about what sort of a person you will be to manage.

Your answer

It's best to avoid going into too much detail and giving too precise a description. Try to keep your answer broad so that it is unlikely to exclude too many people. Horoscopes are carefully written to sound meaningful and yet remain as vague as possible so they can be pertinent to as many people as possible. You want to adopt the same tactic.

By phrasing your answer carefully, you can also score a few discreet points with regard to what sort of a person you are like to work with. Try to convey the impression that you'd most like to work for someone who was a lot like you and then give a positive description of that person.

EXAMPLE

I'd most like to work for someone who has the same approach as I do to getting things done – planning, organisation and action. Also, I'm always keen to take on new duties and responsibilities so I'd welcome a manager who was prepared to give me the chance to continue my professional development. Besides this, a good manager is, of course, always approachable, supportive and sensitive to the needs of their team; whilst I'm good at working on my own initiative, every team needs a leader to give it direction.

Chapter **21**

Illegal questions – and how to dodge them

Whilst it is clear from the previous few chapters that interviewers might question you on a whole range of different subjects, you need to know that they do not have the right to ask you anything they please. There are a number of topics which the law specifically prohibits them from discussing.

The main reason an interviewer will ask such questions is that they are lacking in experience. An HR professional will be well aware of the rules and generally steer clear of such questions. An owner–manager of a small company, on the other hand, might very well be blissfully ignorant that it is illegal to ask such a seemingly innocent question as, 'Do you have children?'

If there wasn't the possibility that you might get asked illegal questions, then I wouldn't have bothered writing this chapter. However, I regret that it is a fact of life that many interviewers will still ask such questions and I, therefore, need to equip you to handle them appropriately.

Effectively handling illegal questions can be tough.

Why are certain questions illegal?

Whilst most questions that an interviewer asks are designed to help discriminate between different candidates, they should be discriminating on the grounds of your ability to do the job. They should not be discriminating on one of a number of different grounds which are deemed to be unfairly discriminatory because they are not relevant to your ability to undertake the role for which you are applying.

What should you do when confronted with an illegal question?

Answering an illegal question is going to be a real test of your diplomatic abilities.

First of all, you face the problem that, depending on how they have phrased their question, it might be hard to establish whether it really is an illegal question or just an inappropriate personal question.

If it is definitely an illegal question and you point out to the interviewer that they shouldn't have asked it and that you have no intention of answering it, I can virtually guarantee that it's going to destroy your chances of getting the job. This is especially so if the interviewer was totally unaware that it was an illegal question, which will generally be the case.

I have the utmost respect for the laws which are there to protect candidates from discrimination. The best solution is going to be for you to answer the question but to aim to sidestep it and steer the conversation away from this particular topic.

TOP TIP

Be aware that just because an interviewer has asked you a potentially discriminatory question, it doesn't necessarily follow that they are prejudiced in any way. It may simply have been a poor choice of question. It is, therefore, important not to take it personally and consequently react in a hostile manner. The interviewer may have betrayed a certain lack of professionalism; don't allow yourself to follow their example.

What types of illegal question might you be asked?

There are a whole host of possible questions you might be asked, which will, to one degree or another fit the definition of illegal. They can be broken down into a small number of key areas: age discrimination, sexual discrimination, racial discrimination, religious discrimination, disability discrimination, discrimination on the grounds of trade union membership, and discrimination on the basis of spent criminal convictions.

I will cover each of these in turn below.

Age discrimination

An interviewer could ask, 'How old are you?', which you might think is a reasonably harmless question, although possibly a little personal. Alternatively, they might elaborate on the question in such a way as to reveal why questioning you on your age is simply not acceptable.

➤ Aren't you a little young to hold a position of this level?
➤ Aren't you perhaps a little old to cope with this job?

These questions might very well make you feel rather uncomfortable, but are they discriminatory?

Are you indeed too young to be able to have a position of such responsibility/authority? Or are you too old to keep up with such a fast-paced role?

Of course not…

William Pitt was just 24 when he became Great Britain's youngest prime minister. He went on to spend 20 years in office during the course of a highly distinguished career.

William Gladstone, on the other hand, was still going strong as British prime minister at the age of 84.

I will admit that these are fairly extreme examples but being prime minister of Great Britain is a fairly extreme job and, whether 24 years old or 84 years old, both these individuals succeeded admirably.

The Equality Act 2010 makes it quite clear that an interviewer should not be questioning you on your age. You should no longer even put your date of birth on your CV.

Whilst an interviewer has the right to make their selection on the basis of experience – which may sometimes favour more mature candidates – they should not rule someone out of the recruitment process on the basis of age.

If you're faced with a question concerning your age, phrase your answer in such a way to demonstrate to the interviewer that your age is not a relevant factor; it is your skills and experience that count. Use this question as an opportunity to reiterate your key selling points and how they match the requirements of the job.

I would note that legislation is always complicated and I have, out of necessity, simplified the interpretations given in this chapter. You should be aware that there are always exceptions to every rule. For example, if you are older than, or within six months of an employer's normal retirement age, then an employer does have the right to reject your application on these grounds. However, most exceptions are fairly minor and will only apply to a very small percentage of individuals.

Sexual discrimination

Whilst it is normally very clear when a question is discriminatory on the grounds of age, sexual discrimination can be a lot less obvious.

Sexual discrimination is normally a greater problem for female applicants; however, it is important to be aware that male applicants can also be targeted. It all depends on the circumstances and the precise line of questioning that an interviewer adopts.

'Are you married?' might seem an innocuous enough question to ask either a man or a woman and it's not actually illegal for an interviewer to ask this. However, it can rapidly lead on to a whole gamut of questions which contravene the Equality Act 2010.

> Do you have any children?

> Do you plan to have any children?

> When do you plan to have children?

> You're not pregnant, are you?

Previously, many candidates would volunteer information about their family on their CV:

Marital status: Married; two children

However, this is now considered a potential invitation to discriminate and it is no longer recommended.

Once an interviewer has established your marital status and whether or not you have children, it may lead them into severely discriminatory territory.

> What impact will the travel requirements of this job have on your family?

> How does your wife/girlfriend/husband/boyfriend feel about you taking this job?

> Is arranging childcare going to cause problems for you?

Your marital status is not relevant to your ability to do the job. Your family is your own private business. What impact this job might have on members of your family and whether taking this job might cause you any problems are issues that you will have to deal with; they have nothing to do with your employer and they don't have any right to be questioning you on such subjects.

When faced with such questions, it's probably not going to be to your advantage to take offence. Try to handle them in a very matter-of-fact manner and, if you can identify your interviewer's concerns, you may wish to address these, but make sure you don't come across as being defensive. The interviewer shouldn't have asked you the question in the first place so you hold the moral high ground.

Besides questions relating to your marital status and your children, it is worth mentioning that there are a variety of other lines of questioning which are deemed to constitute sexual discrimination, including questions regarding your sexual orientation. Whilst these are less likely to crop up in interviews, it has been known.

Racial discrimination

It's important to note that racial discrimination isn't limited to the colour of your skin. Racial discrimination can be a whole lot more subtle than that; it could come down to a simple difference of nationality or even the town or county in which you were born.

It is usually pretty obvious whether or not a question is racially discriminatory.

➤ Where were you born?

➤ Where do you come from?

➤ What is your mother tongue?

These types of questions are normally totally irrelevant and are consequently discriminatory.

Whilst an employer has the right to ensure that you are entitled to work in the UK and is allowed to select on the basis of your ability to communicate in English (or any other language, for that matter) they are not allowed to discriminate arbitrarily on the basis of your geographic or ethnic origins.

Racial discrimination is one of the most widespread and pervasive forms of discrimination and many readers of this book will be painfully aware of that fact.

My advice would be to answer any such questions in a factually correct fashion and to say no more. This isn't a topic you should dwell on.

As I have previously mentioned, the interviewer is not necessarily prejudiced. They might just be curious (and inexperienced).

If, however, you suspect the interviewer is prejudiced in some way, then you need to ask yourself:

➤ Would you really want to work with/for such an individual?

➤ Would you be prepared to take the matter further and make a formal complaint?

These are questions that only you can answer. Personally, I feel that, whilst it may be in your own best interests to let the matter drop, this world needs people to stand up to such behaviour if we are ever to succeed in eradicating it completely.

STATISTIC

A recent BBC investigation revealed that 25 out of 30 recruiters agreed to a request to only send white applicants for a receptionist job. Whilst the job in this case was hypothetical, prejudiced employers most certainly exist and you may well find yourself confronted with one.

Religious discrimination

Discrimination on religious grounds is rare. Whilst religious differences continue to be the cause of conflict, we nevertheless live in an increasingly secular society.

Interviewers are unlikely to question you as to your religious beliefs, largely because the issue is unlikely to cross their minds. The most likely reason for the idea to pop into their heads is if some aspect of your appearance outwardly reveals your beliefs; for example, you might wear a Star of David on your necklace. Religious discrimination is also closely linked with racial discrimination, and if an interviewer has identified a racial difference between you, they may also suspect a religious difference.

The bottom line is that this question is (in almost all cases) completely and utterly irrelevant. It's absolutely none of the interviewer's business.

There is, however, nothing to be gained by getting indignant. My advice would be the same as for a racially focused question; answer factually but don't elaborate. The interviewer will hopefully move swiftly on to other, more appropriate, topics.

Disability discrimination

It is permissible for an employer to question you as to whether or not you have a disability. However, the Equality Act 2010 generally prevents them from taking a disability into account when making their selection. On this basis, one might wonder why they have the right to ask you at interview and why it can't wait until a firm job offer has been made. The reason is that an employer is only obliged to make 'reasonable adjustments' to accommodate a disabled person. If, despite such adjustments, a candidate would still be unable to do the job effectively (as a result of their disability), then the employer is nonetheless allowed to reject the application.

There are various ways in which an interviewer could approach this topic.

➤ Do you have a disability?

➤ How do you cope with your disability?

➤ Can you undertake this job with your disability?

➤ What adjustments would we need to make to accommodate your disability?

However they go about questioning you, your aim should be to briefly disclose the nature of your disability and then go on to detail the adjustments which would be required for you to undertake the role.

Whilst it is uncommon for an employer to discriminate on the basis of a disability itself, the interviewer may have concerns as to the changes that will need to be made. If you are aware of state funding which may be available to support such changes, then you can go a long way towards allaying such fears. You should also reassure them that, subject to these changes, you will be able to undertake the role just as effectively as a non-disabled person.

Trade union membership

Discrimination on the grounds of trade union membership can swing both ways. You could be discriminated against for being a member, and you could be discriminated against for *not* being a member.

Your membership (or lack of membership) of a trade union is not relevant to your ability to perform the job for which you are applying; therefore, any questions on this topic are illegal.

You will be the best judge of how to answer any such questions. It will depend on your individual circumstances. You may feel it is to your advantage to disclose the truth. Alternatively, you may feel it is best to politely decline to answer. Being able to tell the truth is definitely preferable but not if you think it's going to cost you the job.

Criminal convictions

The law does not currently provide a great deal of protection for those with criminal convictions. Whilst some might feel that such individuals don't deserve any protection, this is a very short-sighted attitude. Failure to rehabilitate offenders by helping them to reintegrate into society will inevitably lead to higher rates of recidivism.

Limited protection is afforded by the Legal Aid, Sentencing and Punishment of Offenders Act 2012, which allows for certain criminal convictions to be deemed 'spent' after what is termed a 'rehabilitation period'. If a criminal conviction is spent then you are permitted to conceal it from a prospective employer, and if you have any criminal convictions then it is vital to be aware of what this rehabilitation period is. The Act also makes it unlawful for record-keeping bodies such as the Disclosure & Barring Service to disclose details of such convictions.

However, these general rules do not apply to certain employers and organisations. The rationale is to ensure that employers and organisations offering certain sensitive positions, professions and licences can access an applicant's full criminal history before reaching a decision.

If you are in any doubt as regards your own specific circumstances, then it's always advisable to seek appropriate professional advice.

If you have convictions which aren't yet spent then you are legally obliged to disclose them *if asked* and, as the law stands, a recruiter is not formally prohibited from taking this into account when making a selection.

BLOOPER!

Upon being asked if they had a criminal record, one candidate replied, 'Yes, "Light My Fire" by Will Young!'

Exceptions to the rules: genuine occupational requirements

Whilst there is plenty of legislation intended to prohibit unfair discrimination, I have already made it clear that there are certainly exceptions to the rules.

The most significant of these exceptions is where a 'genuine occupational requirement' (GOR) exists.

In cases where an individual's age, gender, sexual orientation, race or religion is genuinely required for them to be able to effectively perform a role, then an employer is permitted to claim a GOR and discriminate on one or more of these grounds, with the onus being on the employer to demonstrate that the personal characteristic concerned is vital to the role.

For example, whilst your gender should normally be irrelevant to your ability to do your job, it would of course not be unreasonable for an employer looking for someone to work in a female-only spa to request that only female candidates apply for the role. To cite another example, a halal butcher must be a Muslim.

Chapter **22**

Special cases: from school leavers to retirees

The questions an interviewer chooses to ask you will depend on numerous factors. One of those factors is what stage of your career you have reached.

Regardless of your circumstances, the majority of the questions I've covered in this book should be relevant to you. However, there are a few specific cases I'd like to handle in this chapter because they are likely to encompass a significant proportion of my readers, and if you fall into one of these categories, you might be faced with certain specific questions or subtle variations of them for which you need to be prepared.

➤ School leavers

➤ Recent graduates

➤ Changing career path

➤ Returning to work after a career break

➤ Retirees and those approaching retirement.

As always, forewarned is forearmed!

School leavers

If you're a recent school leaver then you definitely qualify as a special case, primarily because you will have little or possibly no previous work experience. You may think this will rule out a number of classic questions interviewers like to pose. However, skilled interviewers will normally be able to rephrase their questions to probe not your work experience but your school record.

'How would your colleagues describe you?' can be turned into 'How would your teachers describe you?'

By switching one word, 'Can you tell me about a major problem at work that you've had to deal with?' becomes 'Can you tell me about a major problem at school that you've had to deal with?'

And 'Can you tell me about the best boss you've ever had?' translates easily to 'Can you tell me about your favourite teacher?'

Whilst these types of questions need a little adaptation, you will find that many of the classic questions can just as easily apply to school life as they can to working life.

➤ Do you work well on your own initiative?

➤ How do you handle pressure and stress?

➤ Can you tell me about a time when you have failed to achieve a goal?

There are also a number of questions which are only ever likely to be asked of a recent school leaver.

➤ What subjects did you most enjoy at school?

➤ What subjects did you least enjoy?

➤ How were your final exams?

➤ What did you normally do during the school holidays?

➤ Why haven't you decided to continue your education?

➤ Wouldn't you like to go/shouldn't you have gone to university?

You need to be prepared for these and to have thought through and perfected your answers just as you would when preparing for any other interview question.

If you don't have any work experience, then the interviewer will be aware of this and if it was a major obstacle to your performing the job they wouldn't be bothering to interview you. If they are taking the time to interview you, then it's because they believe you may have something to offer, and you should draw on your school experiences to help make a compelling case that you do indeed have something to offer.

TOP TIP

Don't be shy. Speak up. And avoid giving monosyllabic yes and no answers if it's at all possible – it nearly always is. Too many school leavers fail at interview because they are simply uncommunicative.

Recent graduates

Recent graduates are also a special case because they are also likely to be lacking in practical work experience, and because they are likely to be subjected to detailed questioning about their time at university.

As with school leavers, most of the standard interview questions can be adapted or rephrased to cope with the fact that you will have little or no work experience. You need to be just as prepared for all the most common questions as any other candidate needs to be. You may have very little in the way of work experience so you will have to construct your answers in light of your university experiences. This isn't a problem, though, as a graduate you have a lot to offer an employer even if you don't yet have any relevant work experience. Is successfully completing a degree course really that different from 'working'?

Besides the generic questions, there are many other questions specific to recent graduates that an interviewer may decide to pose.

In the next chapter we mention the question, 'In what ways is your degree relevant to the work you are now doing?' This could be asked of someone who graduated a year ago or ten years ago. However, for someone who has only just graduated, an interviewer will probably rephrase this along the lines of, 'In what ways is your degree relevant to your ability to do this job?' It's vital to give careful thought to your answer in advance because this one is a favourite among interviewers.

Other popular questions for graduates include:

- ➤ Why did you decide to go to this university?
- ➤ Why did you decide to read this particular subject?
- ➤ What class of degree are you expecting/did you achieve?
- ➤ What aspects of going to university did you enjoy the most?
- ➤ Which module/course/project did you most enjoy?
- ➤ What extracurricular activities did you engage in?
- ➤ How has life at university prepared you for the workplace?

I can't answer these questions for you. It's up to you to apply the principles we have covered so far in this book and produce your own answers. But remember to bear in mind that the interviewer will be assessing your answers in the context of the job for which you are applying. Be positive in your answers demonstrate the drive and enthusiasm which led you to the successful completion of your degree. Your lack of practical experience may be a small disadvantage, but your degree is a powerful selling point.

Changing career path

If you have decided to change your career path, then the main obstacle you face will be your lack of relevant experience. You may have a wealth of experience in the workplace but if it's not directly relevant to the job for which you are applying this will certainly present you with a challenge.

TOP TIP

Make sure you highlight your willingness to learn new skills and to undertake additional training if necessary. Having the right attitude is essential. Be enthusiastic and determined

When formulating your answers you should ensure that your comments remain relevant, and try to focus on the transferable skills and abilities that you have developed.

Interviewers are always going to be curious about a candidate whose career hasn't followed a straight path. You can expect to be questioned on this in a variety of different ways, including:

➤ Why have you decided to change your career path?

➤ What difficulties do you perceive in changing your career path?

➤ How will you be able to compensate for your lack of relevant experience?

➤ What are your key transferable skills and abilities?

➤ Would you say that you're a quick learner?

➤ Why didn't you want to remain in your previous line of work?

➤ What makes you think this line of work will be right for you?

Returning to work after a career break

If you're returning to work after a career break, then this is always going to raise some questions in an interviewer's mind.

We have already discussed sexual discrimination in the previous chapter and established that an interviewer should not be asking you questions about your married life, your children or your future family plans. However, there will be no avoiding the fact that there is a large hole in your CV, which you will be expected to account for (and should already have accounted for within your CV). You may also be affected by other prejudices, most notably ageism.

The main question the interviewer will be asking themselves is why they should be hiring you, rather than someone who is perhaps younger and possesses more recent qualifications and experience. I'm not saying this is fair; I'm simply saying it's important to know that this is what they're thinking because it will help you when phrasing your answers (and even when writing your CV) to know what you're up against.

They may also be worried about the possibility that your family commitments will have a detrimental effect on your work.

➤ Will your working overtime be a problem for your family?

➤ Is it going to be difficult for your family if you have to travel?

➤ How reliable are your childcare arrangements?

They're not really permitted to ask you such questions but, again, you need to keep in mind that this is what they will be thinking and that these are the sorts of objections you are going to need to overcome. By identifying your interviewer's concerns, you are better able to find ways to address these, but make sure you don't come across as being defensive.

Questions they are more likely to ask, and for which you need to be prepared, include:

➤ Why have you decided now is the right time to return to the workplace?

➤ Are you sure a full-time role is the right choice for you?

➤ How do you think the industry/sector has changed since you were last in work?

Of course, there are many other reasons for a career break, including:

➤ Further training/education.

➤ Caring for a family member or close friend.

➤ Travel.

➤ Inability to find a suitable position.

➤ Ill health.

➤ Imprisonment.

For the full story on how to handle these circumstances, please take a look at question 29, 'Why is there a gap in your CV?' in Chapter 20: Forty classic questions you must be prepared for.

Retirees and those approaching retirement

We discussed age discrimination in the previous chapter and established that it is totally unacceptable for interviewers to ask, 'How old are you?'

However, this isn't necessarily going to stop them *thinking* along the lines of:

➤ Aren't you perhaps a little old to cope with this job?

➤ Are you too old to keep up with such a fast-paced role?

They're certainly not allowed to ask such questions, but they may ask you with a variety of other questions, which you need to be prepared to handle.

➤ Have you given any thought to your retirement plans?

➤ At what age are you planning to retire?

➤ Why have you decided to work on past normal retirement age?

The important thing for you to bear in mind is that your age is not a relevant factor; it is your skills and experience that count. Demonstrate these effectively to the interviewer and the 'age factor' will hopefully be forgotten.

Chapter **23**

Yet more questions

I have covered all the most frequently asked interview questions in this book, but there are many other possible questions you could be asked.

It is beyond the scope of this book to analyse dozens of questions in detail, so I will list some of the more important ones for you to read through, think about and draft your own rough answers to.

Once you are familiar with an interview question you will never again be stumped or surprised by it; being surprised in an interview is the last thing you want to happen. Surprise leads to pressure, pressure leads to stress, stress leads to panic and panic can ruin your interview very quickly!

Some of these questions will be variations on the same theme as one or more of the questions I have already covered, and it is up to you to think them through and adapt your pre-prepared answers to fit the circumstances.

Other questions will be completely new and, whilst you are less likely to be asked them, it never hurts to be prepared.

Talking about your current employment

➤ Where does your current employer think you are at the moment?

➤ What are your current boss's weaknesses?

➤ What are your current employer's plans for the year ahead?

➤ Can you tell me what you enjoy about your current job?

➤ What will you remember most about your last job?

➤ Is this the first time you have made an effort to move away from your current employer?

➤ How do you feel about the possibility of leaving your current job?

➤ How would you describe your current employer?

Talking about the vacancy

➤ How quickly can you adapt to a new work environment?

➤ Would it be a problem if we asked you to work overtime/evenings/ weekends?

➤ When would you be available to start?

➤ Do you mind if we contact your current employer for a reference?

➤ Wouldn't you be better suited to working in a larger/smaller organisation?

- How do you feel this vacancy differs from your current role?
- What reservations do you have about your ability to undertake this job?
- Can you describe your ideal working environment to me?
- How do you feel we compare to our competitors?
- What would you say is our unique selling point?
- What would be your analysis of the current trends in our industry/sector?

Understanding your career path, plans and ambitions

- What aspects of your career path would you like to have been different?
- What are your greatest regrets about the path your career has taken?
- What has been the greatest challenge you have faced in your career to date?
- What do you think are your main career options for the next five years?
- What exactly does the word success mean to you?

Addressing problems in your career history

- Why did you stay with this organisation for such a short time?
- Why did you stay with this organisation for such a long time?
- You've been out of work for a while. Has it been difficult finding a job?
- What's your sickness record like?

Coping with stress and pressure

- Are you able to multitask?
- Can you juggle a number of different projects simultaneously?
- How do you handle rejection/disappointment/failure?

Defining teamwork

➤ How do you deal with interpersonal conflict?

➤ What do tact and diplomacy mean to you?

➤ What makes for a successful team?

Management and leadership

➤ Would you describe yourself as a good manager?

➤ How would you describe your ideal team member?

➤ Do you really think you're management material?

➤ What is your attitude to delegation?

➤ Can you give me an example of a time when you had to lead from the front?

➤ Have you ever had to fire or lay off a member of your staff?

Personal and professional development

➤ In what ways is your degree relevant to the work you are now doing?

➤ What have you learned and how have you developed over the last year/five years?

➤ In what ways do you intend to improve upon your performance?

➤ How has your current job prepared you for greater challenges/responsibility?

Your weak points

➤ You must surely have more than one weakness?

➤ What character flaws do you have?

➤ How do you handle being criticised?

➤ What really makes you lose your rag?

➤ How did you cope with the most difficult colleague you've ever had?

➤ Are you able to make difficult decisions and tough choices?

➤ Why haven't you achieved more in your career?

➤ What don't you like about this line of work?

Interests and activities

➤ Do you know what the current headline news is?

➤ What sports are you/have you been involved in?

➤ What book are you reading at the moment?

➤ What newspaper do you take?

➤ Are you interested in current affairs?

The amateur psychiatrist

➤ Describe yourself in three words...

➤ Would you rather know a lot about a little or a little about a lot?

➤ If you were an animal at the zoo, which animal would you be and why?

➤ If you won the Lottery what would you do?

➤ Can you tell me about the best teacher you ever had?

➤ If you could meet any historical figure, who would it be and why?

➤ What are you most afraid of?

Money, money, money

➤ What is your current salary package?

➤ What salary package are you expecting for this role?

➤ Why aren't you earning more?

➤ How much do you think you are really worth?

➤ How much does money matter to you?

➤ Would you still be interested in this job if your current employer offered a pay rise?

➤ Have you ever had to take a pay cut to keep your job?

➤ Have you ever asked for but been refused a pay rise?

Deal making

➤ How would you react if I were to offer you this job on the spot?

➤ See this pen? Can you sell it to me?

➤ What makes you better than any of the other candidates I'm interviewing?

➤ I think you're overqualified for this job. Don't you?

Tough questions: taking the heat

➤ What reservations do you have about working for us?

➤ What do you think of me as an interviewer?

➤ If you were in my position, what questions would you ask?

➤ What would be the toughest question I could ask you?

➤ What do you think the chief executive thinks of the company?

➤ How long is your long term?

➤ What would you do if you caught a member of staff kissing the boss?

Some weird and wonderful questions

➤ If there was a monkey hanging from a chandelier, how would you get it down?

➤ Why don't polar bears eat penguins?

➤ How much water would it take to fill St Paul's Cathedral?

➤ Who would win in a fight between Superman and Batman?

➤ Who is your favourite Doctor Who?

➤ Is a Jaffa Cake a cake or a biscuit?

➤ Do you like to sing in the bath?

➤ Which three celebrities would you like to join you for a night out?

➤ What would you do if the sun died out?

➤ What do you do when there is no answer?

➤ How many dogs in the world have the exact same number of hairs?

➤ How do you fit a giraffe in a fridge?

➤ How many ways can you get a needle out of a haystack?

➤ Would you rather fight a horse-sized duck or 100 duck-sized horses?

➤ If you were an elephant, what would you do with your trunk?

➤ What shapes are best for manholes?

➤ Why is water tasteless?

The Interview Question & Answer Book

It is beyond the scope of this book to cover the questions above in detail, I have covered all 100 of them (and a few more!) in my best-selling book, *The Interview Question & Answer Book: How to Be Ready to Answer the 155 Toughest Interview Questions*. You can place your order for a copy via our website: **www.jamesinn.es**

PART 5

ENDING THE INTERVIEW

Chapter **24**

Your own questions

Interviews are always a two-way process. Not preparing your own questions for the end of an interview is a common and significant interview mistake.

There aren't many interviews that conclude without the candidate being asked, 'Do you have any questions for me/us?' Almost all interviewers will give you a chance to ask questions and you should use this as an opportunity to further demonstrate your interest and enthusiasm. If you don't then you'll come across as passive and uninterested.

> ## STATISTIC
> ....
>
> A recent survey showed that 29 per cent of recruiters stated that the candidate not asking questions or asking poor questions at the end of the interview was sufficient reason for the recruiter to fail them.

What to ask

Don't ask too many questions you're the interviewee, not the interviewer. But do be prepared with a few intelligent questions. Here's a good selection of examples for you:

What is expected of you?

➤ What are the top priorities for my first six months in the job?

➤ What would you expect from me in my first 100 days on the job?

➤ In what ways does this role impact on the growth of the organisation?

➤ How has this role evolved since it was created?

What can you expect of them

➤ How would you describe the team I will be working with?

➤ How would you describe the work culture here?

➤ What do you enjoy most about working here?

Measuring results

➤ How does the organisation measure its success?

➤ In what ways is performance measured?

The future

➤ How do you see my role evolving over the next two to three years?

➤ How do you see the organisation evolving over the next five years?

➤ Are there any plans for expansion?

➤ What scope is there for future promotion?

➤ What training and professional development opportunities will be available?

It's important to phrase your questions as if you had already bagged the job. It's a subtle psychological technique, which will project self-confidence and help further persuade the interviewer that you are the right candidate for the job.

One last sales pitch

If you have not been asked about something which you feel illustrates an important aspect of your ability to do the job, don't be afraid to bring it up yourself at the end of the interview. You could, for example, ask how important such-and-such an ability is to the job. When the interviewer answers that it is indeed important, they've given you the perfect opportunity to roll out a pre-prepared example demonstrating that you have this ability. Just make sure that the ability you choose to discuss is indeed an important part of your job or else you'll come across as somewhat confused about the role!

An advanced technique

Another good question to ask is whether or not the interviewer has any reservations about your application, and if so what they are. It takes a bit of nerve to ask this question. And you had better be absolutely ready to address any reservations they may have; this will probably be your last chance to do so. It might be described as an advanced technique but if you can uncover any possible objections the interviewer might have to hiring you and counter-attack effectively, then it can make all the difference. It's a question which will certainly demonstrate self-confidence at the very least.

Don't ask questions just for the sake of it. One candidate, when asked if she had any questions, replied, 'Are you going anywhere nice on your holidays this summer?' Clearly that didn't make the best of impressions!

Topics to avoid – and what NOT to ask

First of all, avoid questions which the interviewer may expect you to already have the answers to. This includes questions about the organisation, which a quick look at their website could have answered. You'll expose a lack of preparation.

It's also best to avoid questions about pay and holidays, unless, of course, the interviewer brings up these topics themselves. Such matters can always be covered in later discussions. Bringing them up during your interview can place too much focus on what you are expecting from the employer rather than what you are offering them. This is never a good idea.

You should also avoid asking questions which the interviewer is unlikely to know the answers to! They won't take kindly to this at all. Your interviewer may work within a centralised HR department whose staff can't be expected to know the precise operational details of every other department.

TOP TIP
....

Whatever questions you select, be aware that they can reveal a lot about you, the way you think, your motivations, your needs etc. Remember this and try to keep your questions upbeat and positive.

It's hard to give precise advice as to what questions not to ask because it will always depend on the precise circumstances. However, here's a selection of examples which it will generally not be appropriate to ask:

> ➤ How long have you been in business/operating for?
> ➤ Who founded/owns the company?
> ➤ Who are your main competitors?

➤ How is this industry/sector evolving?

➤ What is the salary on offer?

➤ When could I expect a pay review?

➤ How many days paid holiday do I get?

➤ Will I be expected to work overtime?

➤ If I work overtime, will I get time off in lieu?

➤ Is there sick pay?

➤ Do you provide childcare?

➤ What other perks are there in the package on offer?

➤ Are there any non-compete clauses in the contract?

➤ Have you made any redundancies recently?

➤ How did I do?!

➤ Which bus should I get to go to…?

Wrapping up

In wrapping up, make sure you find out when you can expect to hear whether or not you have been successful, it could be anything from the same day (in which case, you may even be asked to wait around for a decision) to a couple of weeks. Don't ever be tempted to ask the interviewer if they felt the interview went well; it smacks of desperation! I heard of one candidate who even admitted to the interviewer that he didn't feel the interview had gone very well and asked if perhaps there were any other jobs going elsewhere in the organisation! Don't let nerves get the better of you.

And finally, remember to thank the interviewer for their time before you leave.

PART **6**

THE 15 MOST COMMON INTERVIEW MISTAKES

Chapter **25**

How to avoid them

The same mistakes crop up time and time again at interview. Too many jobseekers miss out on their dream job because of a small number of easily avoided blunders.

Some of the mistakes people make at interview are very obvious and others are more subtle. The CV Centre® has conducted a comprehensive survey to derive a 'Top 15' and, in this chapter, I will list these 15 interview mistakes and refer you back to previous chapters, where necessary, to explain both why they are a mistake and how to avoid them.

1 Not knowing enough about the job you're applying for

The key to preventing pre-interview jitters is to prepare thoroughly. We fear what we don't know and what we can't control, yet there is so much you can do to plan and prepare for your interview, and the first item on your list should be to thoroughly research the job in question.

Not knowing the ins and outs of a job is among the worst blunders you can make in an interview as is failing to demonstrate to the interviewer how you meet the requirements for the job.

If you are to be able to convince a recruiter that you are right for the role then you obviously need to first get it clear in your own mind why you are right for the role and you can't do this unless you have properly researched and understood what it will involve.

For further guidance on researching for your job, please refer back to Chapter 2: Researching the job.

2 Not knowing enough about the organisation you're applying to

A number of popular interview questions are designed to probe and assess your knowledge of the organisation to which you are applying. An interviewer will expect you to have done your homework. If you're unprepared and unable to answer these questions adequately then it's going to be a big black mark on your application.

Just as a lack of knowledge of the job in question will count against you, a lack of knowledge of the organisation will betray a lack of effort on your part. How can they be sure you really want this job and that you're really the right candidate for the job if you know so little about their organisation?

> **BLOOPER!**
>
> ....
>
> One candidate, famously, upon being asked what they could bring to the company, responded with 'What is it that you do again?'

For further details on what to read up on before your interview, please refer back to Chapter 3: Researching the organisation.

3 Arriving late

The importance of making appropriate travel arrangements to get to your interview may seem obvious. However, this is frequently a problem for candidates. Being late for an interview – even by only a few minutes – is a very common mistake but it will immediately count against you.

> **STATISTIC**
>
> ....
>
> Nearly half of recruiters won't give a candidate a job if they are more than ten minutes late for interview – regardless of how well they perform.

It's important to arrive early to allow yourself time to relax and compose yourself.

4 Lacking enthusiasm

Whilst there's obviously a fine balance here, enthusiasm in an interview is essential – just don't overdo it! Recruiters often find that the person they are interviewing lacks enthusiasm and this will naturally count against you. Sometimes it might just be due to nerves and shyness but don't let this happen to you. Be enthusiastic and show it.

Confident people inspire confidence in others. If you appear confident that you are able to do the job, the employer is likely to be more inclined to believe that you can, showing a lack of enthusiasm is generally fatal to your chances of success.

I talk about this subject in greater detail back in Chapter 5: Mental preparation.

5 Arrogance

Whilst confidence is critical to a successful interview, it is important not to go to the other extreme and appear overconfident or arrogant, which is a surprisingly common mistake. You simply need to appreciate what your strengths are and value yourself accordingly.

Issues such as nerves and confidence are covered in detail in Chapter 4: Mental preparation.

6 Dressing inappropriately

Presentation, presentation, presentation

The way you present yourself physically will make an impression on an interviewer before you even have a chance to open your mouth.

Present yourself professionally and the interviewer will see you as a professional, but the opposite also applies. Never forget that you are marketing yourself, and the way you present yourself can have an impact on the interviewer, almost as powerful as what you actually have to say.

Presentation can make all the difference between success and failure. Image is everything!

STATISTIC

Research has shown that your interviewer could well have made up their mind about you within just 30 seconds of having met you. Use this to your advantage.

I'm not saying you're the sort of person who would wear white socks with their suit, but if you're looking for advice on what to wear to your interview then take a look at Chapter 5: Presentation.

7 Poor body language

Recruiters are trained to make informed assessments of candidates, based on how they communicate verbally and physically.

Even if your interviewer has received no formal training, they are going to be sensitive to certain nuances of body language just like the rest of us. It's instinctive.

The importance of body language as a factor in the decision-making process should not be underestimated. Recruiters regularly complain about candidates' poor body language, limp handshake, lack of eye contact, slouching and failing to smile.

What's all this about body language? Take a look at Chapter 6: Body language.

8 Poor first impressions

First impressions are extremely important. Interviewers can reach a decision about a candidate very quickly; make a poor first impression and you might not be able to recover from it. How quickly do you sum up someone you've just met? It's probably less than a couple of minutes.

Remember: you never get a second chance to make a first impression. Too many candidates turn up reeking of cigarette smoke, garlic or worse! How can you make a really strong first impression?

I help you to answer this question in Chapter 7: The big day, and Chapter 8: First impressions count.

9 Answering the wrong question

It's actually surprisingly easy for your thoughts to stray elsewhere and for you to fail to listen properly to a question. You're in a stressful situation and you have a lot on your mind; it's possible to get distracted.

Interviewers often have to deal with candidates going off at a tangent and giving the answer to a totally different question than the one that was asked.

Listen and engage your brain before opening your mouth!

I talk more about the basic principles of handling interview questions in Chapter 18: Basic principles.

10 Failing to sell yourself effectively

Far too many candidates fail to sell themselves effectively at interview giving boring, monosyllabic answers unsupported by any real-life examples.

It's essential for you to think through and create your own answers to potential questions. Wherever possible, try to integrate real-life examples into your answers rather than just speaking hypothetically. Flagging up specific, relevant examples from your own experience is an ideal way of reinforcing your points in the interviewer's mind.

More about this in Chapter 18: Basic principles.

11 Being a parrot

Many candidates make the mistake of sounding as if they're reciting from an old-fashioned *101 Interview Questions* book.

Make sure you don't fall into this trap. This is really important. There are no universally right answers to interview questions just answers that are right for *you*.

And even if you have prepared and memorised your own answers, you should be careful to make sure that your delivery is natural and doesn't come across as rehearsed.

This important topic is discussed in greater detail in Chapter 18: Basic principles.

12 Lying

Never lie at interview or say something that you cannot substantiate.

For many candidates their troubles start even before they've been invited for the interview. A large percentage of people think it's permissible to tell a few small porkies when writing their CV. It is a fact that many prospective employers do not check an applicant's information as thoroughly as they perhaps should.

However, I would always strongly caution anyone against telling anything but the truth on their CV. You can easily become unstuck during an interview as a result.

STATISTIC

Surveys show that approximately 30 per cent of candidates 'lie' to one degree or another at interview.

For a longer discussion on this topic please refer back to Chapter 18: Basic principles.

13 Being critical of others

Having problems with the boss is the top reason people give (in surveys) for changing jobs. However, you should never say anything negative about either a current or a previous employer.

Criticising your current employer is considered one of the top mistakes you can make at interview and will most likely cost you the job regardless of whether or not your criticism is justified.

BLOOPER!

Having delivered a particularly devastating critique of their current employer, one candidate was rather shocked to discover that their current employer was in fact the interviewer's brother-in-law!

Likewise, you should avoid criticising current or former colleagues.

There are a number of different interview questions you need to look out for on this front.

Question 3 in Chapter 19: The ten questions you're most likely to be asked.
Questions 14, 26 and 27 in Chapter 20: Forty classic questions you must be prepared for.

14 Failing to ask your own questions

Interviews are always a two-way process. Not preparing your own questions for the end of an interview is a common – and significant – interview mistake.

There aren't many interviews that conclude without the candidate being asked, 'Do you have any questions for me/us?' Almost all interviewers will give you a chance to ask questions and you should use this as an opportunity to further demonstrate your interest and enthusiasm. If you don't then you'll come across as passive and uninterested.

STATISTIC
....

A recent survey showed that 29 per cent of recruiters stated that the candidate not asking questions or asking poor questions at the end of the interview was sufficient reason for them to fail.

What should you ask when it's time for you to ask your own questions? Please see Chapter 24: Your own questions.

15 Prematurely talking money

It's best to avoid asking questions about pay and holidays. Such matters can always be covered in later discussions. Bringing them up during your interview can place too much focus on what you are expecting from the employer rather than what you are offering them. This is never a good idea.

Topics to avoid talking about are covered in Chapter 24: Your own questions.

16 Not following up after the interview

Yes, I know I said this chapter would cover the 15 commonest interview mistakes, but everyone loves a bonus, don't they.

So here's a sixteenth mistake for you: not following up after the interview.

And that will be the subject of the next chapter.

PART 7

AFTER THE INTERVIEW: CLOSING THE DEAL

Chapter **26**

Following up

So, you have been to the interview and you think it went well. You should hear one way or the other within a week or so of the interview taking place, unless the interviewer specified otherwise.

But that doesn't mean you should just sit and wait, which is precisely what 90 per cent of people do.

At no stage in your job hunt should you be sitting back and waiting for anything, not until you've achieved the ultimate goal of successfully receiving a job offer. In a tight job market you need to be proactive and constantly keep up your efforts to land a new job.

You need to have a follow-up strategy in place.

What is a follow-up strategy?

Immediately after the interview write (by post or by email) a brief letter to thank the interviewer for their time and seize one last opportunity to make an impact. You want to reiterate how your skills and experience do of course meet their requirements.

So few people take the time to do this that you will stand out in the interviewer's mind possibly at the very moment they are making the crucial decision concerning your future.

It won't guarantee you the job it can only help.

Is it really worth the effort?

The odds are already in your favour if you've been invited for interview. There could easily have been as many as 100 initial applicants. However, fewer than ten are likely to have been selected for interview. Success is within your grasp and one final effort at this stage can really swing things in your favour.

TOP TIP
....

You probably devoted a good hour or two of your time just to attending the interview and yet it doesn't take more than 15 minutes to knock out a well-crafted thank-you letter.

How do I go about this?

Follow up as soon as you can after the interview, either the same day if possible or, at the latest, the next day. By the time a recruiter has reached the interview stage, decisions can be made very quickly. You need to get your final shot in there before it's too late.

If the person whom you originally contacted is not the same as the person who interviewed you, then you should send the letter to the person who actually interviewed you. If you were interviewed by more than one person, then send it to whichever one of them arranged the interview with you (or with the recruitment agency representing you).

> I am writing to thank you for taking the time to interview me on 10 June and to confirm my strong interest in the sales manager vacancy. I would also like to reiterate the qualities which I believe make me ideally suited to the role:

You can follow this introduction with a few key sales points (it is perfectly acceptable to put them down in list form as bullet points).

You can conclude your letter along the lines of:

> I look forward to hearing from you once a decision has been reached. In the meantime, please do not hesitate to call me on 07700 900 159 should you require any further information.

This is a fairly straightforward example and you can, of course, expand on it if appropriate. You may have thought of an important point since the interview which might further support your case. You may be able to refer to something that the interviewer mentioned that was of particular interest. There are numerous possibilities, but don't go over the top; at the end of the day it's only really a thank-you letter.

The Cover Letter Book

If you would like to learn more about such letters then please take a look at my best-selling book on the subject, *The Cover Letter Book: How to Write a Winning Cover Letter That Really Gets Noticed*. You can place your order for a copy via our website: **www.jamesinn.es**

Sometimes you just have to pick up the phone

If a week passes after sending this letter and you still haven't heard anything, then don't be shy to telephone the organisation and enquire politely whether a decision has been reached.

Unfortunately, not all organisations will bother to notify candidates of a negative decision.

Keeping track of your job hunt

We've put together a spreadsheet to help you keep track of the interviews you have attended, who with and what date etc. It will also enable you to keep track of the CVs you have sent out.

Using this tracking tool you will know exactly whether and when to follow up on an application. It will prevent you from becoming confused! It is much better to keep yourself organised. And this Excel spreadsheet will enable you to do just that.

To download your free copy, please visit our website: **www.jamesinn.es**

Chapter **27**

Negotiating the offer

Congratulations! You've got a job offer on the table.

In many cases an employer will make a straightforward offer and you will be inclined to accept it without question; however, there will be occasions when you may wish to negotiate the precise details of their offer. If you're unprepared, this can be a difficult stage to handle. If you've done your research and thought the matter through, your end goal is now very much in sight.

The package

There's a reason this chapter is called negotiating the offer and not negotiating your salary. That's because, depending on your circumstances, there could be a whole horde of other factors you need to take into account besides just your salary.

- ➤ Cash: bonuses; profit share; commission; overtime; staff discounts.
- ➤ Time: holiday allowance, time off in lieu
- ➤ Sickness: sick pay
- ➤ Car: company car, car allowance, car insurance
- ➤ Training: training opportunities, training allowance
- ➤ Medical benefits: private health insurance, dental plan, health club membership
- ➤ Pension: pension plans, pension contributions
- ➤ Childcare
- ➤ Share options
- ➤ Termination: notice period, gardening leave, non-compete clauses

In most cases, salary will be the most important item on your list and will be the main focus of this chapter, but you mustn't lose sight of other factors which constitute the total package. Depending on the nature of any extras, they could make a relatively low basic salary seem much more attractive.

You should also take into account the effect this job is going to have on your CV. If it's going to help you develop in ways that will be of significant value to you in your next job (and will consequently boost your next salary package), then you may be prepared to accept a lower offer in order to secure the job – maybe even lower than you are currently earning.

Market research

The very first step you should take (and should have taken long before a formal offer comes your way) is to research the kind of package usually offered for the type of position for which you are applying. To put it another way, you need to establish your market value. It is vital for you to have a realistic idea of what you should be worth to the employer. Ideally you have this before you even start looking for jobs.

If you're working with a recruitment consultant, they can normally help you with this. However, there is plenty of information to be gleaned through looking at other job adverts and by checking online.

Once you've established a range for your market value, you need to decide:

➤ What is the minimum that you would be prepared to accept, assuming the job is suitably attractive?

➤ What is the maximum you can reasonably expect to achieve without breaking the deal?

Only you can decide what the minimum is that you would be prepared to accept, but your research should make it clear what the maximum is that you are likely to achieve.

The salary question

Although you will need to be specific as to your requirements, it is important (with a few exceptions, e.g. sales and other money-driven and largely commission-based roles) to convey the impression that money is not the only deciding factor in your choice of new job and new employer. Instead, your emphasis should be on politely but firmly conveying that you are aware of your value and that you feel it is only appropriate that you should be remunerated accordingly.

If the prospective employer makes the first move

In most cases the prospective employer will make the first move and tell you what they are prepared to offer. This has both advantages and disadvantages. The main advantage is that the company has shown its hand and you now know how close to (or far from) your own expectations their expectations are. The main disadvantage is that if the offer isn't sufficient then the onus is on you to make the next move.

If you are expected to make the first move

If an employer makes no specific offer but asks you to name your price, then they're putting you on the spot.

Your approach should be to try to identify whether or not they at least have a salary range in mind. An employer will normally have established such a range but, if challenged to reveal it, will probably err on the side of caution, so don't be immediately disappointed if your salary requirements exceed the range quoted.

The next move

Regardless of how the negotiations kick off, you should be aiming to pitch for a salary at the top end of the range and, consequently, be prepared to negotiate and reduce that figure as necessary in order to reach a compromise. This is a standard haggling technique. Start high and be prepared to come down.

Bargaining strategies

The most important bargaining strategy at your disposal is to play this employer off against others. Politely point out that you have applications in progress for other roles where the packages offered are more in line with your requirements, and that you would naturally expect this employer to be able to at least match these offers, if not improve upon them. Whether or not you have firm offers from anyone else is, to a degree, beside the point; the point is to reiterate your market value to the employer and to establish that you expect to receive what you're worth.

If you're unable to adopt this strategy, then your next best strategy is to come clean and state the market research you have undertaken, give the employer the salary range you have identified and then make your case as to why you feel the high end of that scale best reflects your worth.

If you've reached this stage, then you've clearly already made a strong case at interview, and the employer now wants you. This is to your advantage. However, you may still need to make a final pitch to secure the level of salary you desire.

Reaching agreement

Once you've both got your cards on the table, a discussion may follow, and it may take compromises from both of you in order to finally reach agreement.

There are so many different ways in which this conversation could unfold that it's impossible for me to provide you with a precise winning formula. For a start, you may be negotiating in person, via a recruitment consultant, by telephone or even in writing.

TOP TIP

Whatever happens, keep your cool and maintain a professional detachment. Don't let the discussions become heated, and demonstrate to the employer that you are willing to work with them to reach a mutually beneficial agreement. The confident manner in which you handle the negotiations may be sufficient grounds alone for the employer to feel you warrant more than their original offer.

The worst-case scenario

Usually there's nothing to be lost in attempting to negotiate a higher salary than the employer originally offers. Provided you handle the proceedings in a diplomatic fashion, the worst possible outcome is likely to be that the employer sticks to their guns and refuses to contemplate a higher offer. However, having come this far (recruiting is an expensive process) most employers will usually display at least a little flexibility. If they do refuse to budge then it's up to you to decide whether or not their offer is sufficient or whether you will have to reject it. Be warned, if you do flatly reject the offer, the chances of it being increased at this stage will not be high.

Another possible downside to negotiating is if the employer feels they have initially paid over the odds for you, they might be rather ungenerous when it comes to reviewing your salary in the future. However, a bird in the hand is definitely worth two in the bush, and if an employer fails to give you the pay rises you deserve, you can always look elsewhere.

Considering the offer

Once the employer has made their final offer, you are under no obligation to accept it on the spot. It's entirely acceptable – and definitely recommended – to at least sleep on it. Such a major decision requires careful consideration and most employers will respect you for taking a little time to think it over.

Multiple and counter-offers

Another reason for taking at least 24 hours to consider an offer is that it will give you a chance to use this offer to influence others you may have received. If you've worked hard on your job hunt then it's not unusual to get to a position where you are confronted with multiple offers. Whilst there are obvious risks involved, you can attempt to play them off against each other to achieve an even stronger offer.

Bear in mind that it's not just prospective employers who might make you a counter-offer. Your own current employer might well do so. But we'll cover that later in Chapter 29: Resigning.

Get it in writing

Once you have reached a final agreement, it is absolutely essential to get the offer in writing. This should confirm the precise details of the package being offered. It is vital to have this in hand before you contemplate resigning from your current position. I can't stress enough how important this is. A verbal offer can be withdrawn at any time and you could find yourself in a very difficult position.

In the UK there is no legal requirement for a written contract of employment. A contract is deemed to exist the moment you accept a job offer. However, an employer is still required to give you (normally within two months of your start date) what is known as a written statement of employment particulars detailing certain key terms of your employment.

Whilst a written offer on the employer's part is normally legally binding, it is common practice for it to be subject to suitable references. And that is the subject of the next chapter.

Chapter **28**

References

Most offers of employment will be subject to your prospective employer being able to obtain satisfactory references. Indeed, some employers will withhold making an offer of employment until they have checked references.

Of course, not all employers will bother with this formality. With people being increasingly worried about giving anyone a bad reference, the whole references game can often seem a fairly pointless exercise. And it has been known for an individual's current employer to give a glowing reference just because they are keen for them to leave!

Nevertheless, many employers will still pursue references. In certain lines of work they can take the issue of references very seriously indeed.

Who to choose?

You need to choose carefully! Their comments could have a significant impact on your application.

Traditionally, you are expected to be able to provide details of at least two referees – usually one personal (often a former teacher or lecturer) and one professional (usually your current or previous employer). However, it is not unheard of for an employer to want to check not only with your current employer but also with your previous employer and maybe even your employer before that. It all depends on how thorough they want to be and how sensitive a role it is that you are being recruited for.

How to proceed

You could just dish out names and contact details on request, but it is much better etiquette to contact your potential referees before releasing their details. Normally you won't have to worry about this until the interview stage, but some employers will insist on having details of referees up front as will some recruitment agencies.

Generally, it doesn't hurt to start getting in touch with potential referees early. This also gives them a chance to prepare what they will say about you, and gives you a chance to decide if they really are the best choice.

TOP TIP

Details of referees generally shouldn't be included on your CV. They're a waste of valuable space. They clutter it up and, more importantly, you will find that your referees get pestered unnecessarily by time wasters. By the time they have handled their umpteenth enquiry of the day, they are a lot less likely to say nice things about you! A simple sentence saying that references are available upon request is sufficient.

Depending on your relationship with your referee, you may find it is quickest and easiest to just pick up the phone. However, in most cases a brief but courteous letter will be appreciated.

Very occasionally you may be expected to secure a formal written reference yourself, but in the vast majority of cases all you need to do is obtain permission to release your referees' contact details to any interested parties. It's then up to your prospective employer to decide how they wish to proceed.

Chapter **29**

Resigning

There are various different ways of approaching the resignation process – some right and some wrong. You might be leaving your current employer but it never hurts to leave them with a positive impression of you.

There are only two points you really have to get across when resigning.

➤ The fact that you're resigning.

➤ Your acceptance that you are (probably) bound by a notice period.

Anything else is just a nicety.

But it's well worth being as nice as possible about the matter.

Harsh words in a letter of resignation could easily come back to haunt you in the future, not least if you ever need a reference from this employer.

Why are you leaving?

Your employer is going to be wondering why you're leaving. The important thing is to realise that you're under no obligation to go into any details. In fact, you're under no obligation to give any reason at all. You could simply say that you've decided the time is right to 'move on to a new challenge'. Whilst they might be curious to know more, discretion will prevent many employers from prying any further.

Don't burn your bridges

Make the effort to thank your employer for the opportunity they have given you and wish them the best for the future. Keep it very simple and business like, whilst at the same time avoiding being cold and distant. There is nothing to be gained by burning bridges. You certainly shouldn't make any derogatory or disparaging comments about the organisation or any other employee of the organisation.

You may find it hard to resist voicing particular concerns. However, using your letter of resignation to launch a personal attack or to attempt to score points is highly ill-advised, even if your comments are justified. Your intention may simply be to make your employer aware of a particular problem, but such a letter can nonetheless end up sounding vindictive and is unlikely to ever do you any good.

Notice periods

In most jobs you will be bound by a period of notice, stipulated in your contract of employment. You should study your contract carefully so you are aware of precisely what this period of notice is.

You should also identify how many leave days you remain entitled to since these could reduce your notice period.

You are not under any legal obligation to give more than the statutory period of notice; however, in certain circumstances you may wish to do so. If this is the case then this should be made clear in your letter with a statement indicating precisely when it is you wish to leave.

Don't delay!

Resignation letters should generally be sent as soon as possible after you have reached a firm decision to leave. Your decision only becomes legally binding on delivery of your letter of resignation. It should be noted that you don't need to post your letter; email is also legally binding.

Exit interviews

Upon receipt of an employee's resignation, many employers will wish to conduct what is known as an 'exit interview' where they may try to probe your reasons for leaving in greater detail, ostensibly to identify improvements they might be able to make to the working environment or to specific practices and procedures.

TOP TIP

....

As with your original letter, keep your comments at an exit interview professional, not personal. Remember that an employer can't force you to disclose your reasons. Don't let yourself be talked into a corner. Whilst you may have kept your cool in your letter, it can be harder to do so face to face.

Counter-offers

Your employer may try to encourage you to stay with them, so you need to be prepared to face the possibility that you may be offered an improvement to the salary package you currently receive.

You might be very tempted to accept such an offer, so it is important to remember your specific reasons for wanting to resign in the first place. Was money really your main motivator?

You may even be offered a promotion or a move to a different branch or department. This sort of counter-offer will take more serious thought on your part. How does the new job you've been offered compare with the one you are planning to go to?

I'm not saying you shouldn't give serious consideration to counter-offers. I would say that you should proceed with caution.

Rejecting other offers

Besides resigning from your current position, it is also very important to write to politely decline any other job offers you may have received.

This is more than a common courtesy; it is yet another step in building a strong reputation as a serious and professional individual.

Clearly the organisation you're turning down has invested a lot of time and effort in dealing with you. It's going to expect some sort of reason from you for rejecting the offer and you're going to have to give one.

You might have felt your prospective future line manager was cold and distant when you met at interview. You might have felt the salary offer was a joke. You might feel that your future career prospects would be limited within this particular organisation. But is it really going to be to your advantage to tell them any of that? It might make you feel better but it isn't going to do anything to increase your standing in their eyes. You should always be very careful of projecting any negative emotion into a letter.

You should always bear in mind that you might end up dealing with this same organisation again at some stage. If they have made you an offer, then they obviously have a positive impression of you and you want them to maintain that.

Chapter **30**

Handling rejection

It is a sad fact of life that no matter how capable, qualified and experienced you are most interviews will result in rejection for one reason or another. So you had better get used to it! Nearly everybody suffers a few such setbacks when they are hunting for a new job; many Job hunters are regularly shot down in flames. Remember: It just wasn't your destiny.

If you were not successful, try to treat the interview as a learning experience. A real, live interview is the very best form of interview practice you can get. We all make mistakes; make sure that you use them to your advantage for your next interview.

If you had your heart set on a particular opportunity and have been through the highs and lows of being invited to a first interview and then to a second or maybe even an assessment centre, then it can be very demoralising to find out the job went to someone else and all your efforts were for nothing.

Or were they…

Never say never

If you're a philosophical sort of person your initial reaction to receiving a rejection from a prospective employer might be to conclude that it's the end of this particular road and you need to turn your attentions to other possibilities you've got on the go.

However, call me stubborn, but I and many other recruitment professionals still recommend following up on such a rejection with a brief but important letter.

Allow me to explain why.

➤ You have probably worked pretty hard to get to this stage.

➤ They don't want to hire you now but may well be interested in the future.

➤ It should only take you five minutes to fire off this letter.

Building bridges

Having taken the time to build bridges with this organisation, you'd be wise to maintain those bridges as best you can. You never know when your contacts might come in handy later in your career.

➤ You might end up getting a job where you deal on a regular basis with this organisation.

➤ You may have missed out on the current vacancy but there could be another one in just a few weeks' time.

➤ What if the person who won the job subsequently turns it down?

TOP TIP

· ·

Having invested this much in your relationship, it makes sense to seize the opportunity to spend a few more minutes developing that relationship even further.

Maintaining a positive attitude

The way you approach writing this letter is very important. You might feel a degree of resentment for their having made you jump through lots of hoops only to disappoint you, but you certainly don't want that kind of negative emotion to come through in your letter.

There isn't (or at least there shouldn't be) anything personal about the decision: It's just business. You are not being rejected as an individual; your candidature for this particular vacancy is being rejected. In many cases it could be an extremely arbitrary decision; if an employer is faced with a number of high-quality candidates then it can be very hard to choose between them. Indeed, sometimes there is so little to choose between candidates that, more than anything, success or failure is down to luck.

It is fine to express your disappointment but you should definitely avoid sounding bitter. A negative attitude is unlikely to make a good impression.

You should attempt to extract some constructive feedback from them to help you with future applications you make. Most recruiters won't volunteer this information; you'll have to ask for it. You might just get back the usual canned response that 'it was an extremely difficult decision', etc., etc. You might get no reply whatsoever. But you might just get some really useful advice, which could enable you to address any weaknesses or rectify any mistakes so you have a greater chance of success the next time around.

Down but not out

You're also demonstrating that you're somebody who doesn't like to lose and who will do their utmost to make sure they're less likely to lose out again in the future.

Remember: There is a job out there with your name on it; if no one has yet recognised your star quality, it's up to you to dazzle them!

Of course, if you're having difficulty getting yourself invited to interview in the first place, then it may very well be that your CV needs some work.

The CV Book

If you would like to learn more about CV writing, then please take a look at my best-selling book on the subject, *The CV Book: How to Avoid the Most Common Mistakes and Write a Winning CV*. You can place your order for a copy via our website: **www.jamesinn.es**

Chapter **31**

....

Your new job

This is it! There's no turning back now. It's time to bite the bullet! In this chapter we're going to deal with how to successfully get yourself through that all-important first day in your new job.

Your very first day in a new job may not be the most difficult you ever face in that job but you can be jolly sure it will be packed full of challenges. And what are you going to do? Well, you're going to rise to those challenges, of course!

Setting off

On the morning of your first day, make sure that you allow yourself enough time to get ready. And make sure you know where you're going!

It may seem obvious but arriving late on your first day will reflect very badly on you indeed, and it happens all too often. You're most likely going to the same place you went to for your interview but that could easily have been a month or two ago and your memory might be hazy.

Into the spotlight

Your first day is a lot like one big interview. Yes, you've already got the job but people will nonetheless be keeping a very close eye on you until you've settled in. And you may well have an initial trial period to complete before you can really start to feel secure in your new job. There's undeniably a lot at stake but it's definitely no cause for panic.

Depending on the size and type of the organisation, you may have to present yourself to reception on the morning of your first day, or your new boss might be there to greet you personally. When your new boss does turn up, look happy to see them and shake hands firmly but not to the extent that they end up in plaster; shake someone's hand too firmly and they might think you're trying just a little bit too hard.

Whether you feel confident or not, make sure you look it. You might feel like you're back to your first day at school and a little lost. But remember that confident people inspire confidence in others; if you appear confident that you are able to do the job, everyone around you is likely to be more inclined to believe that you can. It's human nature.

First impressions count

First things first, before you get close to doing any actual work, the first thing you'll be doing is meeting and greeting, and first impressions are extremely important. Everyone you meet today will be making initial judgements about you, often on the basis of just a few minutes spent together. Sounds scary? It's not really. It's what you do naturally every day when you meet new people, when you go to a party, for example, or out for dinner with friends of friends. So don't put yourself under too much pressure. But do be conscious of the impression you'll be making on others.

Make sure that you make a powerful first impression on everyone you meet today. Start your new relationships off on a positive foot. Start as you mean to go on.

Start new working relationships

Your relationships with the people with whom you work are immediately going to become the centre of your working life. Building relationships is vital in the workplace. Getting to know the people you'll be working with is one of the most important parts of starting a new job.

In these early stages the most important thing to bear in mind is to take the time to meet people and to make the effort to get to know them. First off, you need to ask for and then remember people's names. (Write them down if it helps.) You then need to find out more about them, start building up a mental file on them.

Avoid talking about yourself too much (what you say could later be used against you by the office gossips and politicians etc.). Be friendly but remain professional. These people are your colleagues, not your friends.

Keep your ears open. Start building up a picture of the various different characters you'll be dealing with and how they interrelate with each other, listening to what they say and how they behave. You should also note the way that your boss interacts with and manages your colleagues, and the way they react with their peers and their seniors. Start to get an idea of just what kind of person they are, what sort of character they have.

Whether you're shy or not, don't be unapproachable; don't be a loner. Get all your new relationships off to an excellent start. Make sure you maintain your level of enthusiasm; it can be tiring and emotionally draining being friendly all day!

251

The little things count too, like saying, 'good morning.' and asking how people are. It's surprising how important these little everyday interactions can be. Don't neglect them.

Not putting your foot in it

It's obviously very important to come across as open and friendly with the people you meet, but keep your guard up. You don't know anything about these people; you don't know their backgrounds, their opinions, their characters; you don't know their relationships with each other. So watch what comes out of your mouth. Think before you speak. Steer clear of saying anything too personal or anything which could be remotely controversial or which could potentially cause any offence to anyone. Tact is the word. Stick to small talk. It can be all too easy to say something which you might later come to regret. Remember: EBBOM – Engage brain before opening mouth!

BLOOPER!

My wife made the big mistake of casually confiding to a colleague that she thought her new boss was 'a bit of a bulldog'. It took less than 24 hours for that boss to find out that their new nickname was 'The Bulldog'!

STATISTIC

It's not just what you say that can count against you. Surveys show that one of the most common errors a new starter can make is accidentally using someone else's coffee cup! People can be terribly territorial.

Bon appétit

Lunch might just be a quick sandwich at your desk or might not exist at all. In many workplaces staff often get together for lunch and there's probably even more chance of this happening if it's your first day. There will probably be at least one person keen to take the new boy or girl under their wing. And that's when you really have to watch what you say! Lunchtime is prime time for gossip and office politics. Don't be antisocial but do play it carefully.

You could turn down the invitation to have lunch together because you have to go down the gym or have some shopping to do or just want to get well away from everyone to clear your head! But be very wary of snubbing anyone on your very first day; your first invitation might well turn out to be your last.

And watch your table manners!

The calm after the storm

After a busy morning when you were very much the centre of attention, you could well find that the afternoon is a calmer affair. Your new boss will probably have run out of people to introduce you to and things to show to you and will hopefully just leave you in peace to settle in.

Seize the opportunity to start getting your workspace organised, throwing out those half-chewed biros your predecessor left behind, and start reading through the inevitable pile of paperwork that will have been dumped on you. There may even be some helpful handover notes left by your predecessor.

You'll probably find it a useful exercise to write up some notes covering all that you've had to learn and take on board so far today. For example, if you're anything like me and have a very poor memory for names and faces, then you might want to jot down the names of the people you've met along with brief descriptions. You can also start preparing a list of gaps in your knowledge and questions you'll want answers to.

TOP TIP

Your brain's probably feeling a little scrambled and it'd be a good idea to 'download' as much information as possible onto paper for future reference.

This should all keep you pretty busy for the duration of the afternoon but you never know you might find time to do some real work! Even if you don't feel you're achieving very much, it's not a great cause of concern; nobody is going to be expecting you to work miracles on your very first day.

Time for tea

It varies from workplace to workplace, but pretty much everywhere I've ever worked tea and coffee drinking have been important tasks! If you're feeling brave then getting up and offering to make or fetch a round of tea or coffee can make a really excellent impression. It might not seem like much but it's a personal gesture which others can hardly fail to appreciate. If you are in doubt as to how the coffee machine works, then don't be afraid to ask a co-worker to show you the ropes. Regardless of whether you're on the bottom rung of the career ladder or at management level, you're showing others that you're one of the team and are happy to muck in.

Final impressions count too

It's time to go home. You're probably pretty tired by now and in just a few short minutes you'll be out of the building and away. But before you do go, make sure you politely bid everyone goodnight, smile and leave with your head held high. First impressions are important, but so are final impressions.

There's a chance you might get asked to join a colleague or two for an after-work drink. If you've got enough energy left then a drink with colleagues might help you to further develop budding new relationships, but you'd probably be wise to limit it to just a couple of drinks! You've had a long, hard day with so much to absorb and assimilate and you're probably not up to capping it off with a long night out.

When you finally get home, it's entirely normal to spend most of the evening thinking back over your first day and pondering on things you could have said or done differently; there's no doubt that you will be more sensitive to any possible slip-ups than anyone else was. But don't beat yourself up too much. Try to get some rest, give yourself a pat on the back and remember that tomorrow is another day!

Ultimate New Job

If you would like to learn more about how to get off to the right start in your new job and not only surviving but actually thriving, please take a look at my best-selling book on the subject, *Ultimate New Job*. You can place your order for a copy via our website: **www.jamesinn.es**

PART 8

MY FIVE TOP TIPS FOR INTERVIEW SUCCESS

Chapter **32**

How to guarantee interview success

If you only have time to read two pages of *The Interview Book*, these are the pages I would most recommend. See them as a cheat sheet, as they encapsulate the most important principles that we have covered in the book. Make an effort to accommodate all these for your interview and you'll immediately be well above average.

1 Be prepared

The key to preventing pre-interview jitters is preparation. If you are to convince a recruiter that you are right for the role, then you obviously first need have it clear in your own mind why you are right for the role. As well as researching the job itself, you should also research the organisation.

2 Make sure you're there on time

Yes, it may seem so obvious yet late arrival is consistently one of the very top reasons cited by recruiters for their rejecting candidates at interview stage. Don't be late. Aim to get there early so as to have time to relax and compose yourself.

3 Create answers to potential questions

It's essential for you to think for yourself and create your own answers to potential questions. Wherever possible, try to integrate real-life examples into your answers rather than just speaking hypothetically. Flagging up specific, relevant examples from your own experience is an ideal way of reinforcing your points in the interviewer's mind.

4 Don't recite your answers parrot-fashion

Too many candidates make the mistake of sounding like they're reciting answers from an interview book. Even if you have prepared and memorised your own answers, you should be careful to make sure that your delivery is natural and doesn't come across as rehearsed.

5 Be confident and show your enthusiasm

Confident people inspire confidence in others. If you appear confident that you are able to do the job, the employer is likely to be more inclined to believe that you can; conversely, showing a lack of enthusiasm is generally fatal to your chances of success. Be enthusiastic, and show it. Confidence and enthusiasm are traits that are guaranteed to impress an interviewer.

Conclusion

Successfully passing an interview is not rocket science! Most of what I have outlined is reasonably simple to take on board; it's just a matter of putting in the necessary time and effort.

I hope you have found *The Interview Book* useful. Don't forget to visit our website: **www.jamesinn.es**

GOOD LUCK!

What did you think of this book?

We're really keen to hear from you about this book, so that we can make our publishing even better.

Please log on to the following website and leave us your feedback.

It will only take a few minutes and your thoughts are invaluable to us.

www.pearsoned.co.uk/bookfeedback

261

Further reading and resources

Recommended books

Borg, J. (2013) *Persuasion: The Art of Influencing People*, 4th edition,
Harlow: Pearson
Borg, J. (2013) *Body Language*, 3rd edition, Harlow: Pearson
Edenborough, R. (2009) *Brilliant Psychometric Tests*, Harlow: Pearson
Fagan, A. (2011) *Brilliant Job Hunting*, 3rd edition, Harlow: Pearson
Hall, R. (2010) *The Secrets of Success at Work*, 2nd edition, Harlow: Pearson
Hodgson, S. (2007) *Brilliant Tactics to Pass Aptitude Tests*, 2nd edition,
Harlow: Pearson
Innes, J. (2015) *The Cover Letter Book*, 3rd edition, Harlow: Pearson
Innes, J. (2015) *The CV Book*, 3rd edition, Harlow: Pearson
Innes, J. (2015) *The Interview Question & Answer Book*, 2nd edition,
Harlow: Pearson
Innes, J. (2012) *Ultimate New Job*, London: Kogan Page
Templar, R. (2012) *The Rules of Work*, 3rd edition, Harlow: Pearson
Williams, R. (2014) *Brilliant Passing Numerical Reasoning Tests*,
Harlow: Pearson
Williams, R. (2014) *Brilliant Passing Verbal Reasoning Tests*, Harlow: Pearson
Yeung, R. (2013) *Confidence*, 3rd edition, Harlow: Pearson

These titles are available from all major bookshops. You can also learn more about them and order a copy from our website: **www.jamesinn.es**

Online resources

I keep my list of online resources online. That way I can keep it bang up-to-date at all times. Please access our website for a wide range of useful links to job sites and other online resources: **www.jamesinn.es**

Index of questions

Index